ACCORDING TO
LUKE

ACCORDING TO

LUKE

THE GOSPEL OF
COMPASSION AND
LOVE REVEALED

A Cycle of Ten Lectures

BY RUDOLF STEINER

With an Introduction and Descriptive Outline
BY ROBERT A. McDERMOTT

Published by Anthroposophic Press
P.O. Box 749
Great Barrington, MA 01230

Copyright © 2001 Anthroposophic Press

Translation by Catherine E. Creeger
Book design and typesetting by White Cloud Press

This work was originally published in German as *Das Lukas-Evangelium: Ein Zyklus von zehn Vortragen, gehalten in Basel vom 15. bis 24. September 1909.* Dornach, Switzerland: Rudolf Steiner Verlag, 1955.

Library of Congress Cataloging-in-Publication Data
Steiner, Rudolf, 1861–1925.
    [Lukas-Evangelium. English]
    According to Luke: the gospel of compassion and love revealed: a cycle of ten lectures / by Rudolf Steiner; with an introduction and descriptive outline by Robert A. McDermott.
        p. cm.
    Includes bibliographical references.
    ISBN 0-88010-488-0
    1. Anthroposophy. 2. Bible. N.T. Luke. I. McDermott, Robert A. II. Title.

BP595.S894 L8513 2001
299'.935--dc21

                                                     2001018172

Printed in the United States of America

CONTENTS

INTRODUCTION

Approaching Rudolf Steiner's Lectures on the Gospel of Luke

ROBERT A. MCDERMOTT

IN EARLY EDITIONS OF Rudolf Steiner's lectures on the four Gospels and the Apocalypse of John, publishers printed a passage from his autobiography in which he distinguishes between his written works (approximately thirty volumes) and his lectures (approximately 6000, in 300 volumes). Since he delivered his lectures in the moment, focusing primarily on his audience, he did not intend these works to be published. Nor did he expect that three generations later (and no doubt for many generations to come) they would be read by anyone irrespective of preparation. After copies of stenographic reports began to circulate widely, Steiner reluctantly gave approval for these highly esoteric lectures to be published without restriction, but with explanatory notes.

In his autobiography, written in 1924, in the last year of his life, Steiner explained that in his lectures certain premises were taken for granted because his audiences, particularly for the Gospels, were familiar with the spiritual-scientific research for which Steiner had been both revered and attacked. He wrote that his audiences had been familiar with certain esoteric premises, including, at a minimum, "the anthroposophical knowledge of the human being and humanity, and of the cosmos in its spiritual essence, as well as what may be called 'anthroposophical history,' told as an outcome of research into the spiritual world."

Now that more than 200 of Steiner's volumes of lectures are available in German and English, and increasingly in other languages, many readers will try to make sense of them without the background that Steiner considered essential for an understanding of his statements. The purpose of this introduction is to provide this background with particular reference to the cycle of ten lectures on the Gospel of Luke, which Steiner delivered in 1909, the fourth of ten lecture cycles on the Gospels that Steiner delivered between 1907 and 1911.

These lectures require that the reader confront the dramatic difference between their contents and the Gospel written by Luke in Greek, perhaps in Rome (where Luke and Paul worked together), probably between 80 and 90 A.D. Some readers will be unprepared for Steiner's account of the differences between the Gospel of Luke (which contains, for example, a visit to the Nativity by shepherds) and the Gospel of Matthew (which speaks of a visit to the Nativity by Magi). Probably all readers not familiar with Steiner will be unprepared for several additional claims introduced in these lectures, including the role of world-historical spiritual figures such as Hermes,

Moses, Elijah, Zoroaster, and Buddha. These lectures also provide an amazing (not to say incredible) account of the individuals whose entwined destinies are described in Luke and Matthew, such as Jesus, Joseph and Mary, John the Baptist, and John the Evangelist.

How might a reader new to Steiner and anthroposophy deal with the astonishing descriptions contained in the ten lectures in this volume? There is no one way that can be said to be best. The karma — that is, the spiritual capacity, receptivity, and aspiration — of each individual will have its own way. The higher self of each reader will no doubt be active to some extent, and no one can know in advance what these lectures will hold for him or her. Nor will anyone know, even after reading, how such revelations will speak to him or her in months or years to come.

In matters of spirit, the best approach involves sound judgment rooted in reverence and humility. As the Buddhist tradition is so prominent in these lectures, we might recommend a Buddhist ideal, the middle way — in this case, between naïveté and skepticism. No one involved in this enterprise — neither Steiner nor the publisher of these discourses nor I in this introduction — is seeking the reader's assent or belief. To some readers, Steiner's statements will seem unhelpful and no advance on one or another exoteric interpretation of the Gospel of Luke, such as that of the preeminent Roman Catholic biblical scholar Raymond E. Brown. For such readers, an easy assent would be of little spiritual value; it would probably be better to accept only what is edifying, leaving the rest to the side.

As often happens, a second reading might have an entirely different effect. Anyone interested in spiritual and esoteric truths would do well to investigate Steiner's teachings, whether concerning his reading of the Gospels or his ideas on education, agriculture, medicine, or the arts, to see what they might offer. The middle way in this case would hold fast between belief based on Steiner's authority and disbelief based on a commitment to long-held and cherished pictures. Such an approach would call for the reader to employ the same spiritual virtues that Steiner considers to be necessary preconditions for progress on an esoteric path — humility and reverence. These preconditions are set forth in Steiner's foundational work *How to Know Higher Worlds* (1904).

Reading these lectures on the Gospels for the first time can be startling because they travel so very far from the usual understanding of the events in the Gospels. Yet the Gospels were also shocking when first read and recited by the early Christians. Now we are used to a certain telling, with familiar words and images. Steiner's account, however, takes the reader behind the Gospel texts. In effect he is recounting the ideas and images of the evangelists — in this case Luke — just as they in turn recounted the events in the spiritual life of Jesus Christ.

When Steiner refers to the "premises" of anthroposophy or spiritual science, he is warning the reader that his "Gospel of Luke" is an esoteric reading of Luke's own esoteric reading. He is not at all focused on the Gospel that has come down to us, and which, he believed, left out much of the esoteric material — including, it would seem, material that Luke either did not formulate in words or omitted, or that did not survive written versions. He also tries to show that each of the four Gospels includes esoteric material presented in words, images, and symbols that modern readers find difficult to decode.

Assuming that Steiner was able to do what he claimed —
render a deeper, hidden description of what Luke actually saw
— how was he able to do this? How was such vision possible?
How could someone in 1910 have access to the visions experienced by a writer of a Gospel two thousand years earlier? The
answer to these questions depends on one's assessment of a
specific phenomenon — the Akashic record, a spiritual light
in which the events and ideas of the past are recorded in their
essential meaning. The whole of Steiner's account of the past
depends on this claim (one that is by no means unique to
Steiner). All esoteric researchers, including, for example, The-
osophists, essentially "read" a light that stores a summary of
the important events, thoughts, and moments of consciousness. Clairvoyance ("clear seeing") consists primarily of reading spiritual realities in this universal record of consciousness.
Such clairvoyant reading is conscious — it occurs neither by
channeling nor in trance.

Imagine, then, the birth of Jesus, which was, according to
Luke, attended by the shepherds. Luke was not present at the
Nativity, and in fact never saw Jesus. Luke wrote his Gospel on
the basis of secondhand reports and earlier Gospels, such as
that of Mark. No one schooled in New Testament studies, including Steiner, disagrees with these facts. In agreement with
scripture scholars, Steiner recognizes that the four Gospel
authors were both aided and limited by the ordinary language
and images of Palestine of the first century A.D. Steiner also
maintains that these authors were clairvoyant: they were able
to see and hear supersensibly the events they described.
Steiner's ten lectures are, in effect, to Luke's consciousness (recorded in the Akashic record) as Luke's original clairvoyant
experience was to the words and actions of Jesus. Luke "read"

the statements and activities of Jesus, and that reading, as it originally happened in the mind and soul of Luke, is recorded, as are all such experiences, in the Akashic chronicle.

Although the ability to read the Akasha is very rare in the modern West, it is not rare in traditional cultures and was not at all rare in the ancient world. This set of ten lectures proceeds from the premise that Steiner could put into words Luke's reading of the events in the life of Jesus. Other volumes of lectures by Steiner proceed from the premise that he could clairvoyantly read the clairvoyant readings, in the Akashic record, of Matthew, Mark, and John and also that he could read the life and teachings of Jesus directly in the Akashic light. These latter disclosures are in volumes of Steiner's lectures such as *The Fifth Gospel* and *From Jesus to Christ*.

Since clairvoyance is a rare and advanced ability, how can readers of ordinary capacity understand and assess Steiner's revelations of extraordinary events, particularly the very significant participation in the story of figures such as Buddha and Zoroaster? Although it can be said truly that karma will answer this question for each reader, it is important to understand that karma does not work in a vacuum, without the particulars of words on a page, the integrity (or trickery) of the clairvoyant, the state of mind of the clairvoyant "reader" at the time, and the quality of the ideas and images.

Each reader needs to determine the extent to which he or she is drawn to the pictures that Steiner reveals. Is it spiritually edifying to picture the host of angels at Jesus' birth as a Buddhist choir? Samuel Taylor Coleridge and Owen Barfield distinguish real imagination — seeing a real or true image, one that requires a level of imagination adequate to the image — from fantasy, or the fanciful picturing that consists of parts generated by and rearranged by intellect. The opposite of true imagination (true imaging) is not fact but false picturing; the opposite of fact is error. Imagination and intellect are different ways of knowing, each valid in its way. Steiner used intellect precisely and effectively (for example, in his doctoral dissertation on epistemology), but he also used imagination and intuition at a very advanced level.

Steiner's picture of Luke's experience (not in this instance Luke's Gospel) is intended to help the modern reader to stand in the presence of pictures that Luke saw spiritually and tried to communicate in words. Steiner also used words — millions of them — and he worked with artists, scientists, educators, and priests in an effort to bring long-lost pictures to modern Western consciousness. He also taught methods by which individuals could develop some of his ability to read Akashic pictures, including those of particular spiritual chroniclers, teachers, and artists such as Plato and Aristotle, Krishna and Buddha, the Gospel writers, Christian teachers such as Paul, Augustine, and Aquinas, Renaissance painters and mystics, and scores of modern historical figures.

Acceptance of the idea of an Akashic record — and of the idea that Rudolf Steiner was one of those rare individuals who was able to read this record and could communicate his reading to groups in lecture halls and living rooms in Europe during the first quarter of the twentieth century — is no guarantee that Steiner's actual research will actually speak to each reader. There can be no such guarantee. These ten lectures will succeed for some and fail for others. But even for those for whom they seem to fail, for those who finish reading with no real affinity for Steiner's revelations, it is still possible that something is gained, namely, an experience of the next step beyond one of the deepest and most loved of all the world's scriptures. As many contemporary exegetes, using social-scientific methodologies, shrink the Gospels and their ability to reveal, Steiner expands and extends their revelation. Both of these levels of readings — the intellectual-exegetical and the clairvoyant-esoteric — afford readers and spiritual seekers the opportunity to locate themselves on a spectrum of self-defining epistemologies and spiritual orientations.

Steiner's lectures on Luke are not intended to replace an experience of the original Gospel. Rather these lectures, like all of his more than one hundred lectures on the Gospels, offer an uncut or nonexotericized version of the life and teachings of Jesus as experienced by the clairvoyant Luke. Luke was also a healer, an artist of images, and a profound and pure interpreter of deep spiritual revelation. Steiner's lectures have some of those same qualities, but on a wider canvas and with a distinctively modern purpose: to enable Western humanity to experience, or reexperience, a picture at once simple and profound, true to the Gospel of Luke as it is known and at the same time far beyond the Luke text. This modern reclamation is more than modern readers expect and perhaps can absorb, and yet — because it is spiritual and true — it might be precisely what is needed to break through the boundaries of modern Western thinking.

In reading Steiner's lectures, it would help to read and reflect on the actual New Testament Gospel of Luke. Steiner's account, after all, is his attempt to read in the spiritual light what Luke actually saw, from which he then created a written account. It is important to remember that both the New Testament in English and Steiner's lectures in English have been translated twice — the obvious translation being from Greek to English and from German to English respectively, but the more remarkable one being from the spiritual light to intelligible events, images, and ideas expressed in words.

Steiner's lectures on Luke give his retelling of the images Luke saw, some of which he translated into Greek words and sentences, and much of which Steiner has translated directly from Luke's experience without comparison to what Luke presumably wrote. All scriptures provide the individual an opportunity to define oneself, however tentatively, with respect to the great spiritual questions. Every Christmas season and every Holy Week, Christians are summoned to respond to the great mysteries surrounding the birth and death of Jesus Christ. Even Christians who have heard and read the Gospel narratives every year for a lifetime remain unaware of the radical contrasts between Luke and Matthew concerning the family, birth, and first years of the life of Jesus. Many Christians, though familiar with the words of all four Gospels, are unaware that both Mark and John make no mention of the birth or childhood of Jesus and begin their Gospels with his ministry. The Nativity is treated only by Matthew and Luke, and the differences between them are profound — so much so that Steiner might be believed when he explains that they are in fact describing two different sets of events.

For Steiner, none of this variety and complexity is accidental. In his view, each of the four Gospels brings a distinctive perspective, capacity, temperament, and emphasis. He is, of course, aware that many other Gospels were written at the same time as these four which have survived and have been granted canonical status. Whereas critics and skeptics who study the New Testament find differences among the four Gospels to be proof of their errancy, for Steiner the opposite is the case. He holds that different souls benefit differently from the great sensitivity of Luke and from the great mystical and esoteric profundity of John. One's opinion about the reliability of these four Gospels, both independently and as a composite set, will depend on one's position with respect to the double process of revelation and inspiration. According to Steiner, Luke brought to the followers of Jesus a series of spiritual pictures that are unavailable in the other Gospel narratives.

Such picturing, with the attribution of knowledge and truth, is precisely what is missing in so much contemporary New Testament scholarship. This is not to say that recent research concerning the historical Jesus, such as that of the Jesus Seminar, is not in the service of truth. This famous — and famously controversial — seminar of some seventy scholars has sought to divide statements and events in the New Testament into those that are valid and evidential (in varying degrees) and those that were imagined (either by the evangelist or by the Christian community as a whole). To the extent that this seminar (and similar scriptural research) does its work diligently, it can only serve to bring the original revelation to a truer and clearer light. Such research, however, has an entirely different purpose and result from Steiner's spiritual-scientific research. To compare properly these methodologies, it is essential to emphasize their respective purposes, presuppositions, and methods.

Steiner's research should be sharply distinguished from both scriptural scholarship and theology. He is analyzing neither the texts nor the histories in which they emerged. Rather he himself is the source of a scripture. As with the initial responses to Matthew, Mark, Luke, John, Paul, and others, some readers are intensely interested in his reports, but most contemporary scripture scholars and theologians tend to be uninterested in his lectures on the Gospels and on Christ. The images that Steiner has transmitted are here presented even though scholars such as John Dominic Crossan and Marcus Borg, prominent leaders of the Jesus Seminar, have recently completed an inspiring group process that has succeeded in separating the statements and events considered historical from those thought to have been generated by imagination.

That done, it is now possible to add Steiner's imagination to those of the evangelists and the faith community. The current lively discussion involves at least three mainstream positions. Literalists and fundamentalists maintain that the Gospels should be interpreted as meaning exactly what they say. The Jesus Seminar and scholars with a similar perspective are eager to understand the scriptures in light of the language and culture of the first century. A third position, predominantly Roman Catholic, reads the scriptures in the light of theology and church teaching.

Steiner's contributions represent a fourth position, a radical alternative to these three. Wishing to focus on neither the history of the first century nor on theology, and clearly not limited by a literal interpretation, Steiner takes inspiration and revelation to another level. For him, the faith community precedes the birth of Jesus and continues through the present, presumably into the far-distant future. In this long evolution, inspiration and revelation were usual in the ancient past, less so at the time of Jesus and in the early Christian centuries, and very rare in modern times. One of the results of this devolution of intuition and imagination has been the separation of knowledge and spiritual experience.

What Steiner sought to establish by his early philosophical work — namely spiritual knowledge, or knowledge by imagination, inspiration, and intuition — contemporary New Testament scholarship relegates to the column of statements and events considered to be nonverified or nonevidential. Admittedly, their goal warrants this split: they are trying to remove unwarranted imagination or fantasy. Steiner would support this effort. But without an explicit reference to the possibility of noetic and inspired imagination, it appears that the Jesus Seminar excludes the possibility of true imagination. Steiner wants to be read as an example of precisely this combination: esoteric truths bequeathed by disciplined imagination free of fantasy.

It would be quite pointless to argue with a New Testament scholar who does not grant the possibility of noetic spiritual experience on the part of the evangelists or of the community who in subsequent generations selected these Gospels as canonical. In Steiner's view, the evangelists were able to know and to communicate statements and events that they had neither heard nor seen, had not read in an earlier account, and had not been told of by a community of believers. Rather they reported what they heard and saw directly in the spiritual light, which did and does still contain the experiences they beheld. In response to contemporary exegetical methodology, Steiner claims to deliver his own accounts of the experiences of the evangelists and experiences that he describes as actually having happened.

Despite their sharp contrasts, the gap between Steiner and contemporary New Testament scholarship need not be mutually exclusive: the Jesus Seminar scholars have employed the criteria of exoteric evidence — specifically linguistic, historical, and anthropological evidence — whereas Steiner offers the results of esoteric evidence. Steiner's research ignores exoteric research, whereas contemporary New Testament research ignores esoteric claims as contrary to linguistic, historical, and cultural evidence. Yet both are valuable.

Both Steiner and the Jesus Seminar radically reinterpret the Gospels — Steiner on the evidence of spiritual science and the Jesus Seminar on the evidence of social-scientific and linguistic science. The more the Jesus Seminar removes, the less conflict remains between the Gospels as previously understood and Steiner's disclosures. But if the Jesus Seminar and other scholars go beyond classifying statements and events by evidence to a general rejection of true, imagined statements and events, the gap between Steiner and the Jesus Seminar will be widened and rendered conflictual.

Steiner set out to undo the influence of Kant, particularly Kant's separation of transcendence and knowledge. Kant argued that it is possible, and even desirable, to affirm the existence of God, immortality, and freedom, but it is not possible to know them. In effect, Kant and all who have been influenced by him, however indirectly, employ a double-truth approach to religion: it is fine to believe so long as belief is not regarded as knowledge. To the extent that scripture scholars classify the Nativity accounts in Matthew and Luke not as true imagination but as fantasy (because they are nonevidential), the words both of the evangelists in their time and of Steiner in the twentieth century will be reduced to pedestrian, humanist, common-sense statements and events. In Steiner's view, great spiritual beings used the symbolic language, metaphors, images and cultural forms of the first century in order to bring into history truths and forces which that era could not express in ordinary language.

The Christ lived in the Palestine of the first century but was not limited to it. The history and language of that period are helpful criteria for understanding the meaning of certain statements and events, but they do not help us to know what to believe about these statements or events. After the Jesus Seminar helps us to know how the faith community of first-century Palestine thought and used words and images, then there can begin, on a surer footing, the task of learning what was working through these statements and events. What was the spiritual reality behind each statement and image? What was the spiritual world revealing and how was it both the result of earlier events and intended to make possible certain future events? This is the kind of knowledge that is not well studied by social science but was superbly exemplified by the evangelists — and, as here claimed, by Rudolf Steiner.

For further explication, the reader may want to consult the Descriptive Outline at the end of this edition. The outlines are designed to be read either as prefaces to each lecture or as commentaries that can be read afterward to illuminate some of Steiner's main points in more detail.

ONE

The Four Gospels in the Light of Anthroposophy

THE LAST TIME WE were together here, we discussed Christian esoteric currents from the perspective of the Gospel according to John.[1] We opened our spiritual eyes to mighty images and ideas by immersing ourselves in that document. On that occasion, I stressed several times that studying the John Gospel, which is unique in the religious history of humankind, reveals Christianity's greatest depths, and I told you that the perspectives acquired through a study of that Gospel are in some respects the most profound possible perspectives. Consequently, many of you who attended either that lecture series or another cycle on the John Gospel may wonder today whether we can augment or deepen those perspectives in any way by considering other Christian documents such as the

Gospels according to Luke, Matthew, and Mark. Knowing that we encounter the most profound Christian truths in the John Gospel, those who prefer not to overexert themselves in theoretical matters may question the necessity of further study of the essential nature of Christianity from other perspectives, specifically the perspective of the Luke Gospel, which we may easily believe to be less profound.

However, anyone who thinks they are making a significant statement by expressing such doubt is severely mistaken, not only because the essence of Christianity is infinitely great and can be illuminated from any number of different perspectives, but also because we can learn a great deal from the Luke Gospel that we cannot learn from the John Gospel, in spite of the infinite depths of the latter document. The profound Christian ideas we encountered in the cycle on the John Gospel do not represent the full depths of Christianity, which can indeed be approached from a different standpoint, as we will do in this lecture series by focusing on the Luke Gospel from the perspective of anthroposophical spiritual science.

We will first consider a few preliminary points that will help us understand what we can gain from studying the Luke Gospel even after plumbing the depths of the John Gospel. Our point of departure will be a fact that becomes apparent when we apply anthroposophical perspectives to even a single line of the John Gospel, namely, that the Gospels were written by individuals with an especially penetrating view of the nature of life and existence. Such people, who are able to see into the depths of the cosmos, are called "initiates" and "clairvoyants." In casual conversation, we use these terms more or less interchangeably, but when we approach deeper layers of spiritual life in our anthroposophical studies, we must distinguish between these two categories of individuals who find their way into suprasensible realms. There is indeed a difference between an initiate and a clairvoyant, although nothing prevents an initiate from also being a clairvoyant, and the reverse is also true, at least to a certain extent. To distinguish precisely between these two types of suprasensible experience, we must recall the three levels of perception that transcend our ordinary perception of the world. These levels are explained in my book *How to Know Higher Worlds.*[2]

The type of cognition that is immediately accessible to us can be described by saying that we perceive the world through our senses and apply our reason and our other soul powers to these perceptions to make them our own. In addition, however, the world can be understood on three other levels. The first is the level of so-called imaginative cognition, the second is inspired cognition, and the third can be called intuitive cognition — if we use the word "intuitive" in its true, spiritual scientific sense.

Who possesses imaginative cognition? Individuals whose spiritual eyes perceive a mighty cosmic tableau of images spread out behind the sense-perceptible world. These images are very different from what we call images in ordinary life. The laws of three-dimensional space do not apply to the images of imaginative cognition, which also have other unique qualities that prevent them from being easily compared to anything in the ordinary sense-perceptible world.

To gain a conception of the imaginative world, consider a plant and imagine extracting its visible element from its solid form, so the plant's colors then float freely in the air. If we simply extricate color from a plant and allow it to float freely, the result is a dead figure that consists of color. The preparatory exercises clairvoyants practice, however, ensure that such a form does not remain dead to them. Instead, it is enlivened by the plant's spiritual aspect just as the plant's material aspect enlivens it in the sense-perceptible world. The resulting free-floating form is not dead but consists of colored light that is inwardly enlivened, glimmering and sparkling in a great variety of ways. Each color then expresses one attribute of a soul-spiritual being that is imperceptible in the sensory world. In other words, to clairvoyants, the colors in a sense-perceptible plant express soul-spiritual beings.

Now imagine a world filled with a myriad of gleaming, constantly changing colored figures. Instead of simply seeing colors, however, as you would if these flickering color reflexes were captured in a painting, you must imagine that they all express soul-spiritual beings. For example, the sudden appearance of a green image indicates the presence of a rational being, while a bright-red image expresses a passionate nature. I could just as easily choose a different example and ask you to imagine a sea of interpenetrating sounds, smells, or tastes, which also express the soul-spiritual beings standing behind them, but for the moment please simply think of the imaginative world as a sea of interpenetrating colors. This world is real and has nothing to do with "imagination" in the ordinary sense of the word. There is nothing illusory about it. It is simply revealed to us through a different mode of perception than the sense-perceptible world.

Within this imaginative world, we encounter everything that underlies the sense-perceptible world and cannot be perceived with our physical senses — entities such as human ether and astral bodies, for example. Imaginative cognition teaches clairvoyants about higher beings from an external perspective, just as you learn about other people from the outside when you pass them on the street. You get to know these people better if you have the opportunity to talk with them. Through their words, they express aspects of themselves that are different from what you see when you simply watch them passing by on the street. For example, you cannot tell whether some of these passersby are filled with pain or pleasure, grief or delight. Their emotional state becomes evident, however, when you speak with them. In the former instance, you experience people from the outside and learn about them without their active participation, while in the latter instance they express themselves to you. The same is true of beings in the suprasensible world.

Clairvoyants, who learn about such beings through imaginative cognition, recognize soul-spiritual externalities, as it were. Those who ascend from imaginative cognition to the level of inspired cognition, however, truly interact with these same beings and hear them express themselves. From within themselves, these beings communicate who and what they are. Thus inspiration is a higher cognitive level than mere imagination, and teaches us more about the beings of the soul-spiritual world.

The word "intuition," if used in its true spiritual scientific meaning rather than in the ordinary sense of any unclear thought that occurs to us, signifies a still higher cognitive level. At this level, we do not simply listen in spirit to what beings tell us from within themselves. Instead, we become one with other beings by submerging ourselves in them. This higher level of spiritual cognition requires us to develop such love for all beings that we no longer distinguish between ourselves and the other beings in our spiritual surroundings. Our own essence pours into the spirit that surrounds us and exists inside rather than outside the other beings with whom we interact. Because this can happen only in the divine spiritual world, the term intuition, which means "standing in God," is fully justified.

Thus imagination, inspiration, and intuition are the three levels of perceiving the suprasensible world. Of course it is possible to acquire all three levels, but an individual may achieve only the level of imagination in one particular incarnation. We call such people clairvoyants, although the spiritual domains that can be reached only through inspiration and intuition remain hidden to them. Nowadays, aspiring esotericists are generally not permitted to ascend to the higher levels of suprasensible cognition without first passing through the stage of imagination. Under modern circumstances it is therefore almost impossible for anyone to omit this stage and proceed directly to the level of inspiration or intuition. This would not be the right way to proceed today, but it could and did occur at certain other times in humankind's evolution. At certain times in human history, the different levels of suprasensible cognition were distributed among different individuals, who possessed either imagination or inspiration and intuition. In certain mystery centers, people learned to open their spiritual eyes and clairvoyantly perceived the realm of imagination, the world of symbolic images. Having become clairvoyant to this extent, these people renounced any further aspiration to inspiration and intuition. As a result, they learned to perceive clearly and precisely in the imaginative world through more intensive training. They became specialists in imaginative perception, so to speak.

This specialization, however, resulted in a specific need.

Anyone who wants to behold the imaginative world while renouncing the possibility of ascending to the worlds of inspiration and intuition lives in a world of uncertainty. If left to its own devices in the boundless, fluid world of imagination, the human soul drifts hither and thither without any specific goal or direction. Inspiration and intuition supply certainty in the spiritual world; they show us where the path leads and where the goal is. Thus, cultures and times in which imaginatively clairvoyant individuals forswore higher levels of cognition always required such individuals to be devotedly attached to a guide who possessed the spiritual-perceptive powers of inspiration and intuition. Without inspired cognition, we cannot know where a path leads or how to reach a goal. Those who cannot acquire such knowledge for themselves must trust in the expert guidance of those who can. That is why so many spiritual paths quite rightly insist that students who have only recently achieved imaginative cognition need an intimate connection to a guru or guide who can supply directions and goals that they cannot provide for themselves.

Conversely, at certain times it proved useful to allow certain other people to omit the stage of imaginative cognition and proceed directly to inspired or even intuitive cognition. Such people renounced the ability to perceive imaginative images of the spiritual world around them and devoted themselves exclusively to impressions of the spiritual world that flow from within spiritual beings. With ears of spirit, they listened as the beings of the spiritual world spoke. This situation can be compared to being unable to see a person you hear speaking from behind a wall. Individuals can indeed renounce spiritual vision in order to proceed more quickly to spiritual hearing, which permits them to know what other spiritual beings express. Regardless of a person's ability or inability to see the imaginative world, if that person's spirit ear hears what beings in the suprasensible world have to say about themselves, we say that such a person is gifted with the "inner word," in contrast to the outer word exchanged by human beings in the physical world. It is quite possible for some people who cannot see the imaginative world to possess the inner word, to hear and convey what spiritual beings express.

At certain times in human evolution, these two types of suprasensible experience worked together in the mysteries. By renouncing one type of perception, seers of both sorts were able to enhance both the clarity and precision of their own abilities and the quality of their interaction in the mysteries. Imaginative clairvoyants were specially trained in seeing the world of images, while others bypassed the world of imagination and underwent intensive training in perceiving the inner word through inspiration. The experiences that resulted from specialized training could then be conveyed by seers of one type to the others. This was possible in times when interpersonal trust was cultivated to a degree that our modern evolution prohibits. Today's human beings do not trust each other enough to be satisfied with hearing others describe images of the imaginative world and subsequently adding what they themselves have learned from inspiration. Our faith in the accuracy of other people's depictions is not strong enough. Although the practice was quite common at certain times in the past, very few modern individuals would be content with developing imagination one-sidedly. At our present stage of development, individuals must be led gradually through all three stages of higher cognition without omitting any of them.

At all levels of suprasensible cognition, we encounter great mysteries related to the so-called Christ event. Imaginative cognition, inspired cognition, and intuitive cognition each have much to say about this central event. Bearing this in mind as we consider the four Gospels, we can conclude that the John Gospel was written from the viewpoint of an initiate who perceived the suprasensible world on all levels of cognition, including intuition. If we look closely at the unique features of the John Gospel, however, we see — as we shall also see in this lecture cycle — that it describes events especially clearly from the perspectives of inspiration and intuition, while its imaginative images are pale and unclear. Leaving aside the lesser imaginative content of this Gospel, we can say that its author conveyed all aspects of the Christ that are revealed to those who possess the inner word and intuition. Because the John Gospel is based on inspired and intuitive cognition, its author essentially describes the mysteries of Christ's kingdom as imbued with the inner word, or logos.

The other three Gospels are different. Of these three authors, Luke expresses himself most clearly. The Luke Gospel begins with a strange little preface saying, in effect, that after many attempts by earlier writers to compile and recount all the stories circulating about events in Palestine, the Gospel writer in his turn has decided to attempt to recount — and these are significant words — the knowledge of those who from the very beginning had been the "eyewitnesses and ministers of the word," to quote the usual translation of Luke 1:1-2.[3] That is, the author of the Luke Gospel intends to convey the statements of eyewitnesses (the term would be better translated as "independent seers") and ministers, or servants, of the word. In the Luke Gospel, the term "independent seers" means people who possess imaginative cognition and therefore have access to the world of images, where they perceive the Christ event. Thus the Luke Gospel is based on the accounts of individuals who were not only specially trained in imagination and able to perceive clearly and exactly, but who were also "servants of the word." This term is significant. Rather than saying "possessors" of the word (that is, of inspired cognition), Luke says "servants" of the word, servants of those with access to the pronouncements of the inspired world but no direct personal access to imaginations. Inspired teachers convey their perception to the servants, who are then able to proclaim it. The servants themselves, however, do not possess the word. Thus the Luke Gospel is based on the accounts of independent seers, of individuals capable of direct personal experience in the imaginative worlds, who have also become "servants of the word" by applying the resources of their inspired teachers to expressing their own visions.

Here again we have an example of how carefully the Gospels are worded and how literally we must understand each word. In documents based on spiritual science, everything is very precise and exact. Modern human beings are often totally unaware of how carefully the words in such documents were chosen.

When we begin the study of any subject from the spiritual scientific perspective, we must remind ourselves that physical documents — in this case, the Gospels — are not the source of anthroposophical knowledge. The fact that an event is described in the Gospels does not necessarily make it true for those who base themselves exclusively on spiritual science. Spiritual scientists gather knowledge not from written documents but from the findings of contemporary spiritual scientific research. As such, spiritual scientific sources consist of what the beings of the spiritual world disclose to contemporary initiates and clairvoyants. In certain respects, modern sources are the same as the sources of earlier historical periods. Thus today as in the past, people with insight into the imaginative world can be called "clairvoyants," while the term "initiates" can be used to describe only those who achieve inspiration and intuition. The terms "clairvoyant" and "initiate" need not coincide.

The content of the John Gospel must be based on the research of an initiate who achieved inspired and intuitive cognition. In contrast, the content of the other Gospels is based on accounts by imaginatively clairvoyant individuals who were not yet able to ascend to the inspired and intuitive worlds. Having made this distinction, we can say that the John Gospel is based on initiation while the other three Gospels (especially the Luke Gospel, as its author himself states) are based on clairvoyance. But because it enlists the perceptions of the most highly trained clairvoyants, the Luke Gospel presents exact images where the John Gospel provides only faded pictures. Let me describe this difference still more precisely. Although it is almost never the case today, it is possible for an individual to be initiated into the worlds of inspiration and intuition while clairvoyance — that is, the understanding of the imaginative world — is withheld. Suppose that such a person then encounters a non-initiated clairvoyant who has access to the imaginative world and can see the entire spectrum of imaginations. A person of the latter type would be able to convey a great deal of information to the non-clairvoyant initiate. The latter, although unable to perceive the imaginative world directly, might in turn be able to explain imaginative visions on the basis of inspiration. Today many people are clairvoyant without being initiates, but the reverse is almost never the case. Nonetheless, it is conceivable that potentially clairvoyant initiates might remain unable to perceive imaginations for reasons specific to their individual cases. Clairvoyants would be able to tell such people much that they did not know before.

We must always stress that anthroposophical spiritual scientific knowledge is derived directly from the sources of initiates rather than from documents like the John Gospel or the other Gospels. Spiritual researchers have access to their source at all times and need not resort to historical documents. When their research is complete, however, we can turn to the documents and compare them to spiritual scientific findings. Modern findings on the Christ event are wonderfully reflected in the John Gospel. The value of this document lies in the fact that its author wrote just like a modern initiate. The voice that resounds across the centuries is the same as the voice that we can hear today.

Something similar is true of the other Gospels, including the Luke Gospel. The images its author presents are not the source of our knowledge of the higher world. We discover this source independently through our own ascent into that world. When we speak of the Christ event, the source of our insight is the great tableau of images and imaginations that we perceive when we focus our inner vision on what happened at the beginning of the Christian era. We then compare these images and imaginations to those depicted in the Luke Gospel. This lecture cycle is intended to show how imaginations achieved by modern individuals compare to the descriptions we encounter in the Luke Gospel. For spiritual research into events of the past, there is only one source, and it does not consist of material records. Stones dug out of the earth, documents preserved in archives, and historical writings (whether inspired or not) are not the source of spiritual science. For spiritual science, the only true source is the everlasting Akashic record, which allows us to understand past events without recourse to physical documents.

Today we can choose between two means of acquiring information about the past. We can look at physical records — historical documents if we want to learn about outer events or religious documents if we want to learn about spiritual circumstances — or we can ask what seers behold when the eyes of the spirit are opened to the everlasting chronicle we call the Akashic record, the mighty tableau where everything that ever happened in the evolution of the cosmos, the earth, and humankind is written in an unchanging script. Aspiring esotericists gradually learn to read this chronicle. Its script is no ordinary script. Imagine past events appearing before your spirit eye — foggy images of Caesar Augustus and all his actions, for example. Everything that ever happened is revealed to spirit vision, and this panorama is accessible to spiritual researchers at any time. They need no material proofs. When they turn their attention to a specific point in the evolution of the cosmos or of humankind, a spiritual image of events of that time presents itself to view. In this way, spiritual vision can roam through ages past. Its discoveries comprise the findings of spiritual research.

What happened in the earliest days of the Christian era? These events can be seen with the spirit eye and then compared to accounts such as those in the Luke Gospel. Having made this comparison, spiritual researchers know that their vision is shared by seers who lived at that time and saw the past in the same way. We can compare what these seers described as their present to what we discover in the Akashic record of their time.

We must always keep in mind that our information comes from spiritual research, not from documents. Discovering the same information in historical documents simply enhances the value of the documents; we judge their truth on the basis of our own research. Documents increase in value as statements of the truth when we recognize the truth from other sources. It would be misleading to describe this situation, however, without pointing out that reading the Akashic record is not as easy as perceiving events in the physical world. Let me use perceiving a specific human being as an example of where the difficulties lie. From elementary anthroposophy, we know that the human being consists of the physical body, the ether body, the astral body, and the I. As soon as we enter the spiritual world, instead of observing the human being exclusively on the physical plane, we encounter certain difficulties. When you see a human being in the physical world, you confront that person's physical, etheric, and astral bodies and I as a unity. Any human being we observe during the waking state unites all these members in a single entity. To observe the entirety of a human being who is not awake, however, we must ascend to higher worlds. We must enter the world of imaginations if we want to see the astral body, which separates from the physical body during sleep. The being we attempt to observe is split into two separate parts. This is where the difficulties begin.

What I will describe next seldom actually happens because observing the human being is relatively easy, but at least this example will help you understand the potential difficulties. Imagine entering a room where a number of people are sleeping. You see their physical bodies lying in bed and — if you are clairvoyant — their ether bodies. Rising up a level, you perceive their astral bodies clairvoyantly. In the astral world, however, the principle of interpenetrability applies — that is, astral bodies pass through each other. It is possible to confuse which astral body belongs to which physical body. Trained clairvoyants are not easily confused in such instances because this type of perception belongs to one of the lowest levels, and people who reach this level are well prepared to distinguish between astral bodies. The difficulties become significant, however, when we observe beings other than human beings in the higher world or when we attempt to track a human being through multiple incarnations rather than only in the present.

To research where the I of a currently living person was in a previous incarnation, you must pass through the world of the devachan to that person's previous incarnation. You must be able to ascertain which I belongs to the individual in question in each of the preceding incarnations. Relating the continuity of the I to the different levels down here on earth becomes complicated. It is very easy to make a mistake when you look for a particular I in earlier bodies. As a general rule, when we enter higher worlds it is not easy to relate all the aspects of a personality to the Akashic record of an individual's earlier incarnations.

Imagine that as clairvoyants or initiates, we assign ourselves the task of determining the physical ancestors of one John Miller, whom we know in the physical world. Let's assume that we must rely on the Akashic record because all physical documents have been lost. We would have to ascertain all of John's physical ancestors — father, mother, grandfather, and so on — on the basis of the Akashic record in order to see how his physical body evolved through heredity. But if we want to investigate John Miller's earlier incarnations, the path we must follow is completely different from the one leading to his physical ancestors. To trace the earliest incarnations of his I, we may need to go back in time through many eras. We encounter two different currents here. The physical body is not a totally new creation because it is descended from its ancestors through the physical line of heredity. The I, too, is not a new entity because it is linked to earlier incarnations.

The same is also true, however, of the intermediary members, the ether body and the astral body. Most of you already know that the ether body is not a totally new entity and that it may have passed through a variety of manifestations. In a previous lecture, for example, I told you that Zarathustra's ether body reappeared as the ether body of Moses. These historical figures had the same ether body.[4] Tracing Moses' physical ancestors would result in one line of descent, but tracing the ancestors of his ether body would result in another line leading back to Zarathustra and other ether bodies.

When we trace the descent of a physical body, an ether body, or an astral body, we must follow a totally different current in each instance. Each member of the human constitution points in a completely different direction. It is true that the present ether body is the reincarnation of an ether body that was formerly incarnated in a different individuality — that is, not the individuality in which the I was previously incarnated. The same is true of the astral body. When we arrive in higher worlds in search of an individual's previous members, these currents separate. Each one carries us in a different direction, and we discover very complicated processes in the spiritual world. To gain a complete understanding of an individual from the perspective of spiritual research, we cannot simply describe him or her as the descendant of physical ancestors, nor can we simply state from which being the present ether body or astral body is derived. We must describe the paths followed by each member until all four converge in the present being, and we cannot trace all these paths at once. One investigator may discover important information by tracing the path of the ether body, while another traces the path of the astral body. Different investigators may place more emphasis on different members and formulate their descriptions accordingly. To those who cannot perceive what a clairvoyant learns about an individual, it makes no difference what they hear because all the aspects they are told about will seem to describe the same phenomenon. To them, an investigator who simply describes the physical personality is saying the same thing as one who describes the ether body, and they will believe that both are describing the being of John Miller.

I hope this illustrates the complexity of the circumstances we encounter when we attempt to describe the being behind any phenomenon in the cosmos — whether a human being or a nonhuman being — from the perspective of the research conducted by clairvoyants and initiates. I needed to demonstrate that only very comprehensive, multidirectional research in the Akashic record yields a clear spiritual view of a specific being.

When we consider the being described by the John Gospel, whether we call him Jesus of Nazareth before the baptism in the Jordan or the Christ afterward, we see an I, an astral body, an ether body, and a physical body. To describe this being completely and from the perspective of the Akashic record, we must trace the paths these four members of the Christ Jesus being followed through human history. Only then will we fully understand this being. A complete and modern spiritual scientific understanding of accounts of the Christ event illuminates the seemingly contradictory accounts in the four Gospels.

I have often said that purely materialistic modern scholarship, which cannot understand that a higher initiate has more profound and penetrating perceptions than others, fails to recognize the great truth and value of the John Gospel. Scholars who are uncomfortable with the John Gospel attempt to impose some sort of harmony on the other three Gospels, the synoptic Gospels. This harmony is difficult to achieve, however, as long as we base it on material events. For example, the life of Jesus of Nazareth before the baptism in the Jordan, which will be the subject of subsequent lectures, is described so differently by two Evangelists, the authors of the Matthew and Luke Gospels, that to a materialistic way of thinking the differences between their accounts are no less significant than the differences between the John Gospel and the other three Gospels.

Consider the facts. The Matthew Gospel describes how the birth of the founder of Christianity is predicted and comes to pass and how wise men from the East follow the star that leads them to his birthplace. Herod's attention is attracted by these events, and the Redeemer's parents flee with the child to Egypt to escape Herod's preemptive measure, the slaughter of the innocents in Bethlehem. After Herod's death, Jesus' father Joseph is told that he can return home, but out of fear of Herod's successor, he settles in Nazareth instead of returning to Bethlehem. If we compare the accounts of the annunciation of the birth of Jesus of Nazareth in the Luke and Matthew Gospels, we find them very different. In one account the birth is announced to Joseph and in the other to Mary. (We will disregard for today the annunciation of the birth of John the Baptist.)

From the Luke Gospel, we learn that the parents of Jesus of Nazareth were originally from Nazareth but were in Bethlehem for the census when Jesus was born. There is no mention of a flight to Egypt. The infant was circumcised eight days after birth and presented in the temple a short time later, when the customary sacrificial offering was made. The parents then returned with the child to Nazareth to live. Then we are told of a strange turn of events. When visiting Jerusalem with his parents, the twelve-year-old Jesus remained behind in the temple, and when they looked for him, they found him surrounded by scholars interpreting the Scriptures. He seemed expert in scriptural interpretation and amazed them with his wisdom and understanding. Then we are told that his parents took the boy home with them to Nazareth, where he grew up, and little more is said about him until the baptism in the Jordan.

Thus we are confronted with two different accounts of the life of Jesus of Nazareth before he received the Christ being. The chief obstacle to uniting these accounts is how to reconcile the story of the family's flight to Egypt and subsequent return with an ordinary materialistic interpretation of the presentation in the temple according to Luke. On the physical level, these accounts appear completely contradictory, but we shall see that spiritual research sheds light on their truth. The three synoptic Gospels (the Gospels according to Matthew, Mark, and Luke) are intended to force us to accept a spiritual interpretation of historical events. We must realize that nothing is accomplished by refusing to think about the apparent contradictions in these documents or by calling them fictitious when reality proves impenetrable.

The Luke Gospel provides an opportunity to talk about issues not raised by the John Gospel, specifically, about events leading up to the Christ being's entry into the three bodies of Jesus of Nazareth during his baptism in the Jordan. Many significant riddles about the nature of Christianity will be solved when we hear what the Akashic record says about the being of Jesus of Nazareth before this event. Tomorrow we will begin to examine the being and life of Jesus of Nazareth on the basis of the Akashic record. We will then be able to ask how what it tells us about the true being of Jesus of Nazareth relates to the account in the Luke Gospel, which is based on the insight of individuals who called themselves "independent seers" and "servants of the word," or logos.

BASEL, SEPTEMBER 15, 1909

NOTES

1. See Rudolf Steiner, *The Gospel of St. John*, eight lectures held in Basel from November 16 to 25, 1907. Hudson, N.Y.: Anthroposophic Press, 1962.

2. Rudolf Steiner, *How to Know Higher Worlds: A Modern Path of Initiation*. Hudson, N.Y.: Anthroposophic Press, 1994.

3. "Eyewitnesses and ministers": this is from the Revised Standard Version. Later translations such as the New English Bible replace "ministers" with "servants," which is a closer translation of the German *Diener.—Trans.*

4. See previous lecture on reincarnation and karma given on February 3, 1909, in Basel. Only incomplete notes of this lecture are available. They were published in GA 109, *Das Prinzip der spirituellen*

Ökonomie im Zusammenhang mit Wiederverkörperungsfragen. Published in English as: Rudolf Steiner, *The Principle of Spiritual Economy in Connection with Questions of Reincarnation: An Aspect of the Spiritual Guidance of Man.* Hudson, N.Y.: Anthroposophic Press/London: Rudolf Steiner Press, 1986.

TWO

The Luke Gospel as an Expression of Love and Compassion

THROUGHOUT THE HISTORY of Christianity, the John Gospel has remained the document that makes the deepest impression on those who steep themselves in the cosmic currents of Christianity. It was the document of choice for all Christian mystics who emulated the personality and being of Christ Jesus as portrayed in the John Gospel. The relationship of Christians to the Luke Gospel has always been somewhat different. This difference is simply another aspect of the difference between the two Gospels that I described yesterday. In a certain respect, the John Gospel was a document for mystics, while the Luke Gospel was always a devotional book for the general public, for simple, good-hearted people aspiring to Christian sensibilities. The Luke Gospel has come down through the centuries as a devotional book. Because this Gospel tells so much about humankind's greatest comforter and benefactor, the savior of the oppressed, it has always been a source of inner comfort for anyone burdened with pain and suffering. To imbue themselves with Christian love, people turned to this book, which describes the power and urgency of love more than any other Christian document. People who were at all aware of the burden of their errors — and who has not felt this burden? — found edification, comfort, and uplift for their encumbered souls by turning to the Luke Gospel, which told them that Christ Jesus sat at table with sinners and tax collectors and appeared for the sake of sinners as well as for the just. Taking in the John Gospel requires a great deal of preparation, but no heart or mind is too petty or immature to receive the warmth streaming from the Luke Gospel.

Thus the Luke Gospel has always been a book for everyone, edifying even the most childlike minds. Human souls that preserve childlike qualities in their later years have always felt drawn to the Luke Gospel. Of all the Christian truths that flowed from the Gospels into the art of painting, the images of the Luke Gospel spoke with greatest urgency to the human heart. For example, the many artistic portrayals of the deep relationship between Christ Jesus and John the Baptist were inspired by the immortal and unchanging Luke Gospel.

If we take in this document from this perspective, we discover its simple, even childlike quality. From beginning to end, it embodies the principles of love and compassion. This childlike quality is nowhere more warmly expressed than in the story of the childhood of Jesus of Nazareth as recounted by the author of the Luke Gospel. We will discover why this is so as we gradually penetrate deeper into this remarkable book.

Today I will need to make many statements that may initially seem to contradict what I told you about the Christ and Jesus of Nazareth in earlier lectures. The explanations that will follow in the next few days, however, will completely resolve these apparent contradictions and reveal the underlying harmony. My first attempt cannot possibly encompass the entire complex truth of the subject, and today I will need to draw attention to an aspect of Christian truth that seemingly contradicts the aspect that I have stated on previous occasions. We must set out on a path that first reveals individual currents of truth and only later demonstrates the harmony among them. Because I deliberately chose the John Gospel as my starting point for various earlier lecture cycles, I was only able to suggest part of the truth of Christianity. That part remains true, as we shall see in the next few days, but our task today is to consider a different part, which is unfamiliar to most of you.

A wonderful passage in the Luke Gospel tells us that an angel appeared to shepherds out in the fields and proclaimed the birth of the "Saviour, which is Christ the Lord." The passage continues, saying that after the proclamation the angel was joined by a "multitude of the heavenly host" (Luke 2:13). Imagine what the shepherds saw as they looked up! Heaven seemed to open, and the beings of the spiritual world were arrayed before them in a mighty panorama.

Now what was the proclamation the shepherds received? It was clothed in monumental words that reverberated through humankind's evolution; over the course of Christian history, this familiar passage has become the emblem of Christmas itself. Translated correctly, the words that resounded from on high to the shepherds meant something like this: "Divine beings are revealed in the heights so that peace may prevail on earth below among human beings imbued with goodwill" (Luke 2:14). We must clearly distinguish between the shepherds' vision (spiritual beings revealing themselves in the heights) and why it occurred at that moment (to allow peace to enter human hearts that are imbued with goodwill). As we shall see, many of the mysteries of Christianity are implied in these words, if correctly understood. Some research is required, however, to illuminate these paradigmatic sayings. In particular, we must consider the accounts clairvoyants receive from the Akashic record. It is important to look with the eye of the spirit at the time of Christ Jesus' appearance on earth and at the spiritual element that entered earth's evolution at that moment. When we trace the historical development of that element, what is it and where does it come from? At that moment, spiritual currents from very different directions converged in humankind's evolution. Over the ages, different worldviews had appeared in different parts of the world, but at the birth of Jesus, they all merged in a central point and expressed themselves in some way in subsequent events in Palestine. What were the goals and purposes of these different currents?

As I indicated yesterday, the Luke Gospel presents the perspective of imaginative cognition, which is expressed in images. The Gospel presents an image of spiritual beings revealing themselves to the shepherds from on high — first one being, or one angel, and then a host of angels. The question is, how do clairvoyants who are also initiates understand this image, which they can reproduce at any moment by searching the Akashic record? What revealed itself to the shepherds? What does the "heavenly host" of angels comprise? Where did they come from?

One of the greatest spiritual currents to flow through humankind's evolution gradually flowed higher and higher, so that at the time of these events in Palestine it could only shine down upon the earth from spiritual heights, as the image suggests. When we begin to decipher the Akashic record in order to investigate the heavenly host that appears to the shepherds, we are guided back to one of the greatest spiritual currents of human evolution. Before its reappearance at the birth of Jesus, this current had last appeared on earth several centuries earlier, in the form of Buddhism. As strange as it may sound, if we trace the angels' revelation to the shepherds back through the Akashic record to earlier times, we come to the enlightenment of the great Buddha. The religion of compassion and love, the great worldview that moved and illumined human hearts and spirits, first appeared in India and still provides spiritual nourishment for a large part of humanity. It was also destined to reappear in the revelation to the shepherds. We understand what the Luke Gospel tells us only when we look — once again, from the perspective of spiritual scientific research — at the Buddha's significance for humankind and the effect of his revelation on human evolution.

We must understand that the Buddha who appeared five or six hundred years before Christ in the Far East was an individuality who had incarnated many times before. The Buddha was able to become who he was in that incarnation only because he had achieved a very high level of development in his earlier incarnations. The oriental term "bodhisattva" is used to designate the cosmic evolutionary level that the Buddha had achieved. At least some of you have heard me discuss the bodhisattvas from various perspectives. I described how the bodhisattvas relate to cosmic evolution as a whole in the cycle

Spiritual Hierarchies and Their Reflection in the Physical World.[1]
I described this relationship from a different perspective in
the cycle *The East in the Light of the West.*[2] Today we will consider the essential nature and significance of the bodhisattvas
from still another angle, and you will soon discover the harmony in these seemingly disparate truths.

The individual who became the Buddha first had to become a bodhisattva — that is, being a bodhisattva is the individual evolutionary step that precedes buddhahood. The
significance of the bodhisattvas can be understood only in the
context of humankind's evolution, so let's approach it from
this perspective. Human beings have not always possessed the
abilities and capacities they possess now. Only a short-sighted
point of view incapable of seeing beyond its own epoch be-
lieves that the abilities people possess today have been present
since antiquity. What humans can do and know changes from
epoch to epoch. In our present epoch, we have developed rational understanding. We quite rightly say that we accept certain truths on the basis of our reason and common sense and
that we can distinguish right from wrong and logic from lack
of logic. It would be a mistake to believe, however, that these
abilities have always been part of human nature. They emerged
only recently, after a long period of evolution. We can now
use them independently, but this has not always been the case.
Just as children are told what to do by their parents and teachers, even adults formerly had to be told what to do by spiritual beings who, although incarnated among humans, had
evolved further through their own spiritual capabilities and
interacted with superior spiritual beings, divine spiritual beings, in the mysteries.

There have always been individualities who incarnate in

physical bodies but are able to communicate with higher beings who do not incarnate. For example, before human beings
acquired the gift of logical thinking and learned to implement
it independently as we do today, they had to obey their teachers. These teachers, although they also possessed no inherent
physical basis for logical thinking, were able to think logically
in the mysteries by communicating with the divine spiritual
beings of higher regions. Before earthly human nature allowed
humans to think logically or act morally, logic and morality
were received from the spiritual world by such teachers, who
then disclosed them to human beings. The bodhisattvas constitute a specific category of beings of superior ability who,
although incarnated in physical bodies, learn from divine spiritual beings and communicate what they have learned to human beings.

The Buddha was a bodhisattva before he became a buddha.
In the earth's distant past, each bodhisattva was given a specific task or mission to fulfill in the higher world, so the
bodhisattva who incarnated as Buddha six centuries before
Christ had a particular mission to pursue through many incarnations. He was assigned this task during the very early
stages of the earth's evolution, even before the Atlantean and
Lemurian times, and he focused exclusively on this one task
from epoch to epoch, conveying as much of its essential nature as the earth was able to receive at each evolutionary stage.
Eventually, each bodhisattva completes his mission. Humankind accepts his gift, transforming the godly faculty he carried down from the heights into an independent human
faculty. Each of these spiritual missionaries reaches a point
when his mission is completed and human beings finally acquire an ability they have been preparing to receive for many

centuries. At this point, the bodhisattva can become a buddha. As a spiritual missionary entrusted with carrying out a particular mission, he incarnates for one final time in a physical human body and then no longer needs to incarnate. This time had come for the Buddha. His mission had led him back down to earth repeatedly, but when he achieved enlightenment as a buddha, his final incarnation as a bodhisattva began. He incarnated in a human body that had developed the utmost level of certain faculties that were initially taught from above and were evolving into independent human faculties.

When a bodhisattva's earlier development permits him to perfect a human body so that it develops the particular faculties related to his mission, he no longer needs to incarnate. From then on, he influences humankind from spiritual realms, promoting and guiding human affairs from above. Human beings then accept the task of continuing to develop the faculties that formerly streamed down to them from heavenly heights, the faculties first perfected in a human body by the bodhisattva during the incarnation in which he became a buddha. To be a buddha means to demonstrate the accomplishments of a bodhisattva in the person of one human being by fully incorporating faculties that formerly streamed into human nature from the heavens. This is what the Buddha personified. If, as a bodhisattva, he had renounced his mission at an earlier stage, human beings would never have known the benefits of these gifts from the heights. Evolution progressed to the point where these faculties could be exemplified by a single human, thus sowing the seeds for all human beings to acquire the same faculties in the future.

Until he becomes a buddha, a bodhisattva-individuality does not incarnate completely into a human body but maintains contact with the heavenly heights. When such an individuality incarnates fully into a human body, it is totally absorbed by its incarnation and no longer retreats from it. This incarnation — the buddha incarnation — grants humankind a specific quantity of faculties that must then be further developed by independent human beings. After becoming a buddha, the bodhisattva being is allowed to retreat from the earth and remains visible only to a certain type of clairvoyant perception. He continues, however, to guide human affairs from the spiritual heights.

What was the task of the wonderful, mighty individuality we ordinarily call the Buddha? To discover the esoteric task or mission of the Buddha, we must realize that human cognitive ability developed gradually. I have said repeatedly that in Atlantean times many human beings were clairvoyant and could perceive spiritual worlds. Aspects of this old clairvoyance persisted into post-Atlantean times. Moving from the Atlantean period through the ancient Indian, Persian, Egypto-Chaldean, and even the Greco-Roman cultures, we find that many people — many more than we imagine today — had inherited certain aspects of the ancient clairvoyance. The astral plane was open to these people, and they beheld the hidden depths of existence. For many people, seeing the human ether body was still quite normal in Greco-Roman times. They were especially likely to see the human head surrounded by an etheric cloud, although admittedly this cloud was gradually concealed within the head as time progressed.

But humankind gradually had to perfect sensory cognition, which is acquired through our physical senses and sense-based mental faculties. Gradually, human beings had to descend completely from the spiritual world and acquire merely sensory modes of perception and rational, logical thinking. We had to pass through this non-clairvoyant mode of cognition as a transition to a future stage when we will once again acquire clairvoyant cognition but will unite it with the sensory and rational cognition we have gained as modern human beings. We are living in this stage at present. We look back on our clairvoyant past and forward to a time when human beings will become clairvoyant again. In this transition stage, however, most of us are restricted to what we perceive with our senses and comprehend through reason and common sense.

To be sure, there are different degrees of sensory perception and rational cognition. Some people, who understand very little about morality in their present earthly incarnation and develop little compassion toward their fellow human beings, exist on a lower moral level, while others, who pass through this life without developing their intellectual forces to any great extent, occupy a lower intellectual level. We know, however, that human cognitive forces can achieve much higher levels. All kinds of intermediate stages exist between the lowest moral and intellectual level and the level Fichte calls "moral genius," where moral imagination is developed to the highest possible extent. Moral genius represents the current apex of human perfection, and we know that we can aspire to it without possessing clairvoyant powers, simply by ennobling the forces available to ordinary modern human beings.

Throughout the earth's evolution, humankind worked to achieve successive moral and intellectual levels. Today our independent intelligence and our personal moral strength allow us to recognize, at least to a certain extent, the need to have compassion for the pain and suffering of others. In the distant past, human beings could not acquire this ability for themselves. Today we know that a healthy sense of morality leads to the insight that compassion is the highest virtue; we recognize that humanity cannot progress without love. Even without clairvoyance, we know that we will continue to enhance the sense of morality that allows us to achieve this insight. If we look back in time, however, we realize that we have not always been able to achieve such insight independently.

In the past, because human beings could not realize for themselves that compassion and love are the highest developments of the human soul, spiritual beings such as the bodhisattvas had to incarnate in human bodies. These beings received the active power of compassion and love from higher worlds and conveyed it to human beings, whom they taught to act accordingly at a stage when independent human forces were not mature enough to recognize the need for compassionate and loving behavior. Today, our independent forces allow us to recognize the great virtues of compassion and love to which our sense of morality aspires, but for epochs and epochs we human beings still had no insight into the nature of compassion and love, and these virtues had to be instilled in us from above by the bodhisattva who spent his final incarnation as the Gautama Buddha.

Before becoming the Buddha, this being was the bodhisattva who taught us love, compassion, and all related virtues. Through all the epochs when human beings were still naturally clairvoyant to some degree, this teacher incarnated into clairvoyant human bodies. During his incarnation as the Buddha, he looked back on his earlier incarnations with all the inner feelings of a human soul looking into the depths of existence that lie concealed behind sensory appearances. He had acquired this clairvoyant ability in earlier incarnations and brought it with him when he was born into the Sakya clan of his father Suddhodana. When he was born to Suddhodana and Mayadevi, the person we usually call the Buddha was still a bodhisattva, a being who evolved by reincarnating. He had acquired a high degree of clairvoyance, which he experienced already in childhood.

We must understand that this clairvoyant ability to see into the depths of existence had gradually assumed very specific forms in the course of humanity's evolution. The mission of human evolution required the gradual extinction of the gift of ancient, dim clairvoyance. The inherited remnants of ancient clairvoyance that persisted were not its best aspects. The best aspects were lost first. What persisted was often a lower level of perceiving the astral world, namely, the ability to perceive demonic forces that drag human beings into a lower sphere of drives and passions. Initiation enables us to perceive not only the spiritual forces and beings associated with the most beautiful human thoughts and sensations but also the spiritual powers that stand behind chaotic passions, wild sensuality, and consuming egotism. The clairvoyant powers that persisted in most circles — not among initiates, but in the great majority of people — revealed the wild, demonic forces that underlie lower human passions. Those who cultivate the ability to perceive the spiritual world can see all this for themselves; it is simply a matter of developing human capabilities. But it is impossible to acquire the ability to perceive the spiritual forces of good without also perceiving the forces of evil.

As a bodhisattva, the Buddha naturally had to incarnate into a typical human body of his times — in this case, a body that enabled him to behold the astral depths of existence. As a child he was already able to perceive all the astral figures that underlie wild and stormy passions and greedy, consuming sensuality. Confined to the palace, coddled and spoiled in accordance with prevailing biases about what was appropriate for a child of his class, he was shielded from the sight of the outer world's pain, torment, and physical depravity. His very isolation, however, fostered his inner perceptive abilities. Although he was carefully sheltered and protected from anything that might hint of pain or illness, his spiritual eye was open to astral visions, which surrounded him with images of all the wild passions that can degrade human beings.

This state of affairs is suggested even by what remains of the exoteric biography of the Buddha, if it is read with the eye of the spirit, with true esotericism. I must emphasize again that many statements in exoteric accounts remain incomprehensible as long as we are unaware of their esoteric foundations. This is especially true of accounts of the life of the Buddha. To orientalists and other scholars, it must be strange to read that the Buddha was surrounded in the palace by "forty thousand female dancers and eighty-four thousand women," as we are told by the cheap booklets available today. People do not know that these descriptions of the Buddha's harem, which do not seem particularly surprising to the authors, point to astral circumstances that the Buddha experienced with all the intensity available to a human heart. From his earliest childhood, being shielded from the pain and suffering of the physical human world made him all the more able to perceive the workings of spiritual forces in the higher world. The bodies available to souls incarnating at that time supported such perception, but from earliest childhood the Buddha was invulnerable to its effects. In his earlier incarnations, as he worked his way up to the heights of bodhisattvahood, he strengthened himself against the terrible illusory images and learned to rise above them. But as a bodhisattva individuality in this particular incarnation, he felt a powerful urge to discover the physical manifestations of the astral images that surrounded him in his palace. It was as if each single image urged him to leave his prison and see the world. This was the driving impulse in his soul, because as a bodhisattva he possessed advanced spiritual powers associated with his mission of teaching humanity the full force of love, compassion, and all related virtues. To accomplish this mission he had to get to know human beings in the physical world, where their moral sense would permit them to experience his doctrine of compassion and love. It was absolutely necessary for him to learn about humanity in the physical world in order to evolve, as a human being among human beings, from bodhisattva to buddha. He could accomplish this mission only by renouncing all the faculties he had acquired in earlier incarnations, by moving out onto the physical plane to dwell among human beings and embody the essential human attributes of compassion and love.

Of course many intermediary developments are required; the transformation from bodhisattva to buddha does not happen from one day to the next. The young man felt driven to leave the palace. We are told that when he first broke out of his palatial prison, he met a very old man. Until then, he had been surrounded exclusively by images of youth and had been led to believe that life held only youth's forces of abundance. For the first time, he encountered age on the physical plane. Next he encountered a sick person, and then a corpse, so he learned about disease and death on the physical plane. For the first time, the realities of the physical plane truly confronted his soul.

Legends are sometimes more true than any material scholarship, and one legend in particular is very characteristic of the Buddha. When he left the royal palace, the horse he drove was so grief-stricken by its master's desire to leave his birthright that it died of sorrow and was transformed into a spiritual being and transported into the higher world. This image expresses a profound truth. It would take us too far afield to explain in detail why a horse is used as an image of a human spiritual faculty, but let me remind you of how Plato uses holding a horse's reins as an image of certain human faculties that are still supplied from above and have not yet developed independently within the human being.[3] When the Buddha left the royal palace, he left behind all the faculties that had not yet developed independently in the human soul. He left them behind in the spiritual worlds from which they had always guided him. These faculties are symbolized by the horse that dies of sorrow and is transported into the spiritual world when abandoned by its master.

The Buddha, however, only gradually became what he was meant to be in his final incarnation on earth. He first had to learn about aspects of life on the physical plane that he previously knew only from a bodhisattva's spiritual perspective. In this context, he met two teachers — one representing the ancient Indian worldview known as Samkhya philosophy, the other representing yoga philosophy — and immersed himself in what they had to offer. Even such an exalted being must exert himself to find his way into the outer world that humanity has mastered, and although a bodhisattva learns faster than an ordinary person, he still needs to learn. If he were born today, the bodhisattva who lived approximately five or six centuries before Christ would still have to struggle like a schoolchild to learn what had happened on earth while he lived in the heavenly heights. Thus the Buddha also had to learn about what had happened since his last incarnation. Learning about Samkhya and yoga from these teachers gave him his first glimpse of the worldviews that solved life's riddles for many people of that time, and he experienced firsthand the feelings of souls influenced by these worldviews.

Samkhya allowed him to absorb a subtle, logical, philosophical view of the world, but the more he immersed himself in it, the less it satisfied him. In the end, it seemed like a ghost deprived of any life or vitality. He sensed that the sources that would support what he had to do in this incarnation lay in something other than the traditional Samkhya philosophy.

The second philosophy he encountered was the yoga of Patanjali, which seeks a connection to the divine through specific inner soul processes. The Buddha immersed himself so deeply in yoga that it became part of his own being. It too left him unsatisfied, however, because he realized that it was simply a legacy of the past and that people needed to develop new faculties, such as independent morality. Having put yoga philosophy to the test in his own soul, he realized that it could not serve as the source for his mission at that point.

Next he kept company with five hermits who attempted to reach the mysteries of existence by strictly disciplining, castigating, and denying themselves. The Buddha tested this path but saw that it too could not serve as his source. For a time, he subjected himself to the same self-denials and mortifications as the monks and fasted to eliminate greed and awaken the higher forces that were said to lead quickly from the human bodily element to the spiritual world when the body is weakened by fasting. Because of the developmental level he had already achieved, however, the Buddha recognized the futility of self-castigation and fasting. As a bodhisattva, he had already brought his physical body to the highest level of development possible for human beings at that time. For the same reason, he was also able to experience what human beings must endure on this path to spiritual heights.

Anyone who pursues Samkhya or yoga to a certain level, aspiring to the pure heights of the divine spirit through logical thinking without first acquiring the sense of morality the Buddha had already achieved, encounters a specific temptation. The Buddha subjected himself experimentally to what is called "temptation by the demon Mara." At a certain point, the aspirant is possessed by all the devils of arrogance, vanity, and ambition. The Buddha was familiar with this temptation. The figure of Mara, the demon of vanity and ambition, stood before him, but as a bodhisattva the Buddha recognized the demon and was invincible against him. He knew that if people who were not bodhisattvas continued to pursue self-development in the old way, without introducing the new doctrine of love and compassion and acquiring an independent sense of morality, they would succumb to the demon Mara, who implants all the forces of arrogance and vanity in human souls. The Buddha experienced this temptation personally as he endured the ultimate consequences of the Samkhya and yoga philosophies.

Among the hermit monks, however, he had a different experience. In an attempt to distract human beings from the spiritual world, the demon appears in a different guise to show them all the material goods they might possess — "all the kingdoms of the world" in their glory, so to speak (Luke 4:5–6). The demon Mara approached him, saying, "Do not be tempted to leave everything you possessed as a king's son; go back to your royal palace!" The Buddha learned that the path of self-castigation itself leads to this temptation, to which any other human being would have succumbed, but the Buddha's development allowed him to see through the tempter. He learned what would happen to humanity if people continued to live as before, seeking the path to the spirit only through fasting and self-denial. He himself was invincible against temptation and therefore able to recognize the great danger inherent in attempting to enter the spiritual world by material means without the strong foundation of an independent sense of morality.

As a bodhisattva, the Buddha approached these two thresholds in human development, which non-bodhisattvas would do well to avoid. We might translate his message into ordinary human language as follows: "The highest knowledge is glorious and beautiful, but if you fail to approach it with an innocent heart, a noble mind, and a purified character, the devil of arrogance, vanity, and ambition will attack you." His second lesson is: "The tempter will approach you from the other direction if you attempt to enter the spiritual world by material means, either by self-castigation or fasting, without first appropriately purifying your sense of morality." These are the two teachings of the Buddha that illuminate our modern age. When he was still a bodhisattva, the Buddha revealed the essential aspects of his mission, which had always been to instill a sense of morality in human beings when they were not yet able to develop it independently.

After recognizing asceticism as a danger to humanity, the

Buddha left the five hermits. He began to contemplate, in ways suitable for modern times, the human faculties that can be developed without the ancient clairvoyance that is a legacy of the past. He contemplated these faculties until he achieved the utmost that humanity would ever be able to accomplish through them. In his twenty-ninth year, after abandoning one-sided asceticism, he spent seven days in contemplation under the *bodhi* tree. During this time, great truths were revealed to him, the great truths that are disclosed when human beings seek to learn the fruits of contemporary human faculties in silent contemplation. The great doctrines of the so-called Four Noble Truths were revealed to him, along with the great doctrine of compassion and love that he later taught in the form of the eightfold path. Today I will simply describe these doctrines as an outline of the moral significance of the purest teachings of compassion and love. When they were revealed under the *bodhi* tree, when the Indian bodhisattva became the Buddha, the doctrines of compassion and love entered humanity as independent human faculties for the first time. Since that time, people have been able to develop within themselves the capacity for compassion and love. This is the essence of the Buddha's life and work. Shortly before his death, the Buddha said to his closest pupils, "Do not be sad that the master is leaving you, for I am leaving something behind. I am leaving you the law of wisdom and the law of discipline, which in the future will replace the master." This simply means that the bodhisattva who had taught the content of these laws had achieved the goal of his incarnation on earth and was allowed to withdraw. A faculty that humanity had formerly learned from a bodhisattva had entered the hearts of individuals, where it would continue to develop into the religion of compassion and love. This faculty first entered a human heart during the seven days of contemplation when the bodhisattva of ancient India became the Buddha, and the Buddha subsequently taught it to his pupils in many different forms, which we will consider in a later lecture.

Today we looked back on events that took place six centuries before Christ, because without tracing developments in the Akashic record leading from the Buddha's sermon at Benares to events in Palestine, we would not understand either the path of Christianity or the author of the Luke Gospel, its preeminent chronicler. Once the bodhisattva became the Buddha, he no longer needed to return to earth. Since then, he has existed as a purely spiritual being, influencing events on earth from the spiritual world. As the most important event in earthly evolution approached, an individuality appeared in the spiritual heights to shepherds out in the fields and delivered the proclamation we know from the Luke Gospel. With the angel, there appeared "a multitude of the heavenly host." What was this host?

The image that appeared to the shepherds was the transfigured Buddha, the spiritual figure of the bodhisattva of ancient times, the being who had brought the message of love and compassion to human beings for millennia. Now that this being had completed his final earthly incarnation, he hovered in spiritual heights and appeared to the shepherds beside the angel who proclaimed what was to happen in Palestine.

We learn this from spiritual research, which shows us the transfigured bodhisattva of ancient times hovering above the shepherds. And the Akashic record also tells us that a child was born in the "city of David" to a couple — or at least to a father — who was descended from the priestly branch of the house of David. I must emphasize that this child had been chosen to be illumined and imbued from birth with the strength that had radiated from the Buddha ever since his ascent to spiritual heights. With the shepherds, we gaze at the manger where Jesus of Nazareth, as he is usually called, was born; we see the aura that hung over the child from birth and know that the image of the halo expresses the power of the bodhisattva who became the Buddha, the power that formerly streamed toward human beings and now influences humanity from the spiritual heights. This power worked toward the greatest event of all time as it shone above the child of Bethlehem and prepared him to take his rightful place in the evolution of humanity.

When the individuality who radiated strength toward the infant descendant of David was born in ancient India, a wise old man named Asita perceived the power that we described today. He saw it first in the spiritual world, and it impelled him to go to the palace of King Suddhodana to seek the infant bodhisattva. On seeing the infant, Asita foretold his mighty mission as the Buddha. To the great disturbance of the child's father, Asita predicted that the child would become a buddha instead of ruling his father's kingdom. Asita then began to cry, and when asked whether misfortune would befall the child, he answered, "No, I am crying because I am so old that I will not live to see the day when this savior, the bodhisattva, will walk the earth as the Buddha." From the perspective of that lifetime, Asita's weeping was all too justified because he did indeed die before the bodhisattva became the Buddha. Asita was reborn as the personality described as Simeon in the Luke Gospel's account of the presentation in the temple (Luke 2:25-35). As this Gospel describes, "the Holy Spirit was upon"

Simeon when the child was brought to him. This is the same individuality who, in his life as Asita, cried because in that lifetime he would not live to see the bodhisattva become the Buddha. Now he was granted the gift of seeing that child's next stage of evolution. "Inspired by the spirit" as he entered the temple, Simeon could perceive the aura of the transfigured bodhisattva hovering over the infant Jesus of the house of David at his presentation in the temple. Simeon knew there was no longer any need to cry, because he was seeing what he had not lived to see in a former lifetime. He saw his transfigured savior hovering above the infant and said, "Lord, now let thy servant depart in peace."

BASEL, SEPTEMBER 16, 1909

NOTES

1. Rudolf Steiner, *The Spiritual Hierarchies and Their Reflection in the Physical World: Zodiac, Planets, Cosmos*. New York: Anthroposophic Press, 1970 (GA 110. Düsseldorf, April 12–22, 1909, *Geistige Hierarchien und ihre Widerspiegelung in der physischen Welt. Tierkreis, Planeten, Kosmos*; ten lectures and two question-and-answer sessions).

2. Rudolf Steiner, *The East in the Light of the West, with Children of Lucifer* (by Edouard Schuré). Blauvelt, N.Y.: Garber Communications, 1986 (GA 113, Munich, August 23–31, 1909, *Der Orient im Lichte des Okzidents. Die Kinder des Luzifer und die Brüder Christi*; nine lectures and some remarks on the Goethe Festival).

3. Cf. Plato's dialogue *Phaedrus*.

THREE

Buddha's Contribution to Humanity

W HEN WE FIRST TAKE IN the Luke Gospel, we merely sense its power. We dimly feel that it reveals truly great and mighty spiritual worlds. After what we heard yesterday, we can understand why this is so: spiritual research shows that the Buddhist worldview and all its gifts to humankind flowed into the Luke Gospel. In fact, a unique form of Buddhism, comprehensible to the simplest and most naive hearts and minds, issues from this Gospel.

From what I explained yesterday and will clarify further today, you will gather that Buddhism as such, the teachings of the great Buddha as they first appeared on earth, is a worldview that can be understood only by those who have achieved certain exalted ideas in the pure ether heights of the spirit. A great deal of preparation is required in order to understand Buddhism itself. The Luke Gospel, however, contains the spiritual substance of Buddhism in a form accessible to all human souls who are receptive to the most essential human ideas and concepts. We will be able to explain how this is possible when we fathom the mystery of the Luke Gospel. Nearly six centuries elapsed between the Buddha's enlightenment and the birth of Jesus, and in the interim the hard-earned spiritual accomplishments of Buddhism, which now flow from the Luke Gospel, were enhanced or raised to a higher level. Let's reflect on a few examples of how Buddhism is enhanced in the Luke Gospel.

Yesterday we called Buddhism the purest doctrine of compassion and love. From the Buddha's activity, love and compassion streamed toward all beings on earth. A gospel of love and compassion is evident in true Buddhism, like a warm heart sharing all the suffering encountered in the material world of living things. In Buddhism, we encounter love and compassion in the fullest sense of the words. What flows from the Luke Gospel, however, is more than all-encompassing compassion and love. The Luke Gospel moves from compassion and love into pertinent and urgent deeds. While Buddhists aspire to compassion in the truest sense of the word, Christians who emulate the Luke Gospel aspire to active love. Buddhists share the pain of the sick, but the Luke Gospel calls for active intervention and — to the extent possible — healing. Buddhism allows us to understand what moves and enlivens the human soul, but the Luke Gospel issues a remarkable challenge to refrain from judgment, to do more than is done for us, to give more than we receive. Although we encounter Buddhism in its purest, truest form in the Luke Gospel, it is enhanced and elevated by the transformation of love into action.

This aspect of Christianity, or of Buddhism enhanced by Christianity, is best described by the warmhearted author of the Luke Gospel. Of all the Evangelists, Luke, having been a physician, was most able to understand Christ Jesus as the healer of body and soul and to find profound words that speak to the heart. The particular emphasis of Luke's account of the life of Christ Jesus, which is due to his own experience as a healer of bodies and souls, will become ever more apparent as we plumb the depths of the Luke Gospel.

Another striking aspect of the Luke Gospel is its ability to move even the most childlike hearts and minds. Remarkably, the Buddha's lofty teachings, which are comprehensible only to mature intelligence and seasoned human soul faculties, appear rejuvenated in the Luke Gospel, as if emerging from a fountain of youth. Buddhism strikes us as a mature fruit of the tree of humanity, but in the Luke Gospel we rediscover it as a flower of youth, and we wonder how this rejuvenation occurred. We will find the answer only by looking closely at the teachings of the great Buddha himself. Our anthroposophical preparatory work will permit us to examine, through the eyes of the spirit, what moved his soul.

First let us keep clearly in mind that the Buddha evolved from a bodhisattva, that is, from an exalted being who perceived the mysteries of existence. As a bodhisattva, the Buddha participated in the entire evolution of humankind in ancient times. When human beings reappeared in post-Atlantean times and established and developed the first post-Atlantean culture, the Buddha was already there, serving as a mediator between human beings and the spiritual worlds, as I described yesterday. He was already present in Atlantis and even in Lemuria. The very high level of development that he had achieved allowed him to gradually recall, during his twenty-nine years as a bodhisattva in his final incarnation in India, all aspects of his earlier lives, all of his previous associations. He looked back on his own participation in humankind's evolution and on the gifts he brought down to human beings from divine spiritual worlds. Yesterday I indicated that even such exalted individualities must recapitulate, if only briefly, what they learned in previous lives. Even the Buddha described his bodhisattva period as a gradual ascent toward spiritual enlightenment, toward ever more perfected spiritual perception.

We are told how he described this process to his disciples. To show them the path his soul had traveled in the quest to remember the experiences of earlier incarnations, he said: For me there was a time, oh you monks, when an all-encompassing glow shone toward me from the spiritual world, but I could distinguish nothing — no figures and no images. My enlightenment was not pure enough. Then I began to be able to see not only light but also individual figures and images within it, but I could not yet distinguish what these figures and images meant, for my enlightenment was not pure enough. Then I began to recognize that spiritual beings expressed themselves in these images and figures, but I could not yet distinguish which kingdoms of the spiritual world they belonged to, for my enlightenment was not yet pure enough. Then I learned to recognize which kingdoms of the spiritual world these individual spiritual beings belonged to, but I could not yet distinguish either the deeds that earned them their place in the spiritual kingdoms or their states of mind, for my enlightenment was not yet pure enough. Then there came a time when I could distinguish not only the deeds that had elevated these spiritual beings to the kingdoms they occupied but also their states of mind, but I could not yet distinguish which spiritual beings I myself had lived with in earlier times or what I had done in their company, for my enlightenment was not yet pure enough. Then came a time when I was able to identify not only the beings in whose company I had spent a particular epoch but also what I had done with them. I knew what my previous lives had been, for now my enlightenment was pure.

This is how the Buddha described his gradual acquisition of knowledge that had to be reacquired in each incarnation according to the conditions of that epoch. In his present incarnation, the way he acquired this knowledge had to conform to his complete descent into a physical human body. When we contemplate the Buddha's description, we sense the significance and greatness of the individuality who incarnated as the son of the king from the Sakya clan. The Buddha also knew, however, that ordinary people, with the kind of perception available to them then and in the near future, would have to renounce the world he had learned to perceive. Only initiates like the Buddha himself were able to behold the spiritual world; normal human beings lost this possibility as the remnants of ancient clairvoyant perception grew ever smaller. The task of the Buddha, however, was not simply to speak about what initiates knew. Above all, his task was to speak about the forces that were meant to flow from independent human souls. It was not enough for him to point to the results of his own enlightenment; he had to talk about what ordinary human beings could accomplish by continuing to develop their own inner nature as it was constituted at that time. In the course of the earth's further evolution, human beings would gradually begin to hear the Buddha's teachings speaking to them from their own hearts, from their independent rational minds. The Buddha was the first to state these teachings as a matter of purely human knowledge, but much time would pass before all human souls would mature enough to acquire this knowledge independently. While the Buddha was the first to extract this ability from the depths of human consciousness, others would have to develop it later.

Let's consider another example. Today people internalize the rules of logical thinking in adolescence, and logical thinking is a universal human ability that develops within the individual. But only the great mind of the Greek thinker Aristotle could allow this faculty to emerge for the first time from a human breast. We must distinguish between being the first to extract a faculty from the depths of human consciousness and doing so after humankind has cultivated that faculty for some time.

The Buddha's message was among the greatest teachings ever received by humankind. Only the great heart and mind of a bodhisattva, an exalted and illumined being, could transform this message into a matter of direct human experience. Although all human beings would eventually develop the exalted doctrine of compassion, love, and all the related virtues in their own souls, only the most illumined being could be the first to do so. Consequently, the Buddha had to clothe his message in words that were familiar to the human beings of his time and place. As we have already heard, the philosophies of Sankhya and yoga were taught in ancient India during the Buddha's life time. These philosophies supplied the Buddha with familiar terms and expressions in which to clothe the new teachings that lived in his soul. Although he gave these ideas and concepts totally new forms, he had to use them because any evolutionary step must allow the future to build on the past. Thus the Buddha clothed his sublime wisdom in the familiar expressions of contemporary Indian teachings.

We must attempt to grasp how the Buddha himself experienced the teaching that humanity would eventually internalize. What thoughts can even approximate the profound soul experiences that passed through the Buddha's heart and mind as he sat under the *bodhi* tree during the seven days of his enlightenment? His thoughts ran somewhat as follows: In very early stages of human evolution, many people possessed a dull and dim clairvoyance, and in still earlier times everyone was clairvoyant. Being clairvoyant means being able to use one's astral organs. If we use only the organs of the astral body, however, we sense and feel the most profound mysteries but cannot behold them. Clairvoyant perception begins only when astral experience leaves an impression on the ether body. In ancient times, human beings possessed a dull form of clairvoyance because they were still able to use the organs of the ether body, which at that time had not fully penetrated the physical body. Over time, human beings gradually accepted the loss of the use of their etheric organs and learned to rely exclusively on the physical body's material organs to transmit thoughts, sensations, feelings, and ideas to the astral body.

All this passed through the great soul of the Buddha. He knew that human beings had lost the use of their etheric organs and that the astral body allowed them to experience what the instruments of the physical body transmitted from the outer world. Then the Buddha asked himself an important question. Under normal circumstances, when the eye senses the color red, when the ear hears a sound, or when the sense of taste has an impression of flavor, these sensations are transformed into mental images and experienced in the astral body. If we experienced them in no other way, they would not normally cause pain and suffering. If we simply surrendered to the impressions of the outer world that affect our senses, to the impressions of colors, light intensity, sounds, and so forth, we would make our way through the world without experiencing pain and suffering as a result of such impressions. We experience pain and suffering only under specific conditions. The great Buddha then proceeded to investigate the causes of pain and suffering, sorrow and worry. When do impressions of the outer world become painful? Why do they become painful under certain circumstances?

The Buddha realized that when we look back into ancient times, we discover beings who worked from two directions on the inner nature of human beings — that is, on the human astral body — during our earlier earthly incarnations. During incarnations in the Lemurian and Atlantean periods, the so-called Luciferic beings worked on human nature, and as time passed, their impressions and influences were absorbed into the human astral body. Beginning in Atlantean times, humans were also influenced by beings under the leadership of Ahriman. Thus in previous incarnations people were influenced by both the so-called Luciferic and the so-called Ahrimanic powers. If these beings had not influenced us, we would never have acquired freedom, free will, or the ability to distinguish between good and evil. From a higher standpoint, it is fortunate that we were influenced by these beings, but in a certain respect they forced us to descend more deeply into sensory existence than we would otherwise have done as we left the divine spiritual heights. The great Buddha was aware that human beings had incorporated certain influences that are the legacy of both Luciferic and Ahrimanic activity. We carry these influences within us; they began in earlier incarnations and persist even today.

When the dimly clairvoyant human beings of ancient times beheld the spiritual world, they saw the harmful influences of Lucifer and the influences of Ahriman in the astral world and could distinguish precisely where they came from. Their clairvoyant abilities enabled people of those times to make allowances for such influences and protect themselves against them. They also knew how they had come into contact with those beings. At one time — so said the Buddha — people had known the source of the influences they had carried with them from one incarnation to the next since ancient times. Knowledge of the Luciferic and Ahrimanic powers was lost, however, along with the ancient clairvoyance; since people were no longer clairvoyant, they no longer knew what influenced their souls from incarnation to incarnation. Earlier clairvoyant knowledge was replaced by lack of knowledge, and human beings were overcome by darkness. Although we carry the influence of Lucifer and Ahriman as they did, we no longer know the source of this influence. We carry with us something that we know nothing about. Of course it would be simplistic to deny that something is real and effective simply because we know nothing about it. The influences that entered us over the course of our incarnations are still at work. They are still there; they remain effective throughout our life, but we know nothing about them. This is what the great Buddha realized.

How do these influences work in human beings? Although we cannot recognize them, we feel and sense them. There is a force within each of us that comprises all the aspects of the self that persist from incarnation to incarnation, culminating in our present existence. We fail to recognize the true nature of this force. It is our desire for material life, our longing for worldly perception, our thirst or desire for life. Thus the old Luciferic and Ahrimanic influences continue to work in human beings as the thirst for existence, or the desire to exist, which persists from incarnation to incarnation. This is approximately what the great Buddha said, although he explained it to his closest pupils in greater detail.

To understand the Buddha's descriptions of his experience requires a certain amount of spiritual scientific preparation. We know that after the I and astral body leave the ether body and the physical body at death, we experience a great tableau, a single mighty image, of memories of our life. We know that most of the ether body is then discarded like a second corpse, leaving behind an extract or essence of itself, so to speak. We carry this extract with us through kamaloka and the time we spend in the devachan, and then bring it back with us into our next existence. During kamaloka, however, all our deeds that require karmic compensation are inscribed on this etheric extract that persists from one incarnation to the next. This extract of our previous ether body contains everything that persists from one incarnation to the next; we carry it with us when we reenter earthly existence at birth. In oriental literature, what we call the ether body is usually called *linga sharira*. Thus what we carry from one incarnation to the next is an extract of *linga sharira*.

The Buddha then asked his disciples to consider human beings who have just been born. Burdens remaining from earlier incarnations are inscribed in the *linga sharira* that they bring with them. In our current epoch, we know nothing about its contents, which are hidden from us by the darkness of ig-

norance. As soon as we enter earthly life, these contents assert
themselves as the thirst for existence, the desire for life. The
Buddha saw the so-called desire for life as everything that originates in earlier incarnations and drives human beings to covet
enjoyment of the world, to actively desire the material world
instead of remaining unattached observers of its colors, sounds,
and other sensory impressions. This tendency or force in human beings comes from earlier incarnations. The Buddha's
pupils called it *samskara*. The Buddha told his closest disciples
that people of the present are typically unaware of this important element within themselves. Ignorance transforms this
element, which we would otherwise recognize as coming from
Luciferic and Ahrimanic beings, into the thirst for existence
and all the dark, dormant forces persisting from earlier incarnations. The character of our thinking — the fact that objective thinking is not a matter of course for human beings in
this epoch of evolution — is due to these forces, which the
Buddhist tradition calls *samskara*.

Please note this subtle distinction between objective thinking, which has only its object in view, and thinking influenced
by forces from the *linga sharira*. When you develop opinions,
to what extent are they based on your liking for the object of
your consideration and to what extent on objective observation? In Buddhist terms, truths acquired not through objective thinking about a subject but as the result of old inclinations
from earlier incarnations form an "inner thought organ." This
organ consists of everything we think as a consequence of
specific experiences in earlier incarnations. Remnants of these
experiences persist in the *linga sharira*. In each human being,
the Buddha saw an inner thought organ formed by the total-
ity of *samskara*. He said that this thought substance, and it

alone, causes the development of the current individuality, which Buddhism calls *namarupa*, or "name and form." A different philosophical school of thought calls it *ahamkara*.

The Buddha told his pupils that in ancient times, when human beings still clairvoyantly perceived the spiritual world that underlies physical existence, everyone saw the same thing, because the objective world is the same for all. But when the darkness of ignorance spread over the face of the earth, people began to develop individual potentials that distinguished them from each other. Each individual became a being with a soul of a specific form, and each had a distinguishing name, or *ahamkara*.

The inner consequences of our earlier incarnations possess "name and form," or individuality, and shape our so-called six organs — *manas* and the five sensory organs — from the inside outward.[1] Please note, however, that the Buddha did not say that the eye, for example, is formed exclusively from the inside outward. He said that the eye incorporates an element that is contained in the *linga sharira* and comes from previous levels of existence. For this reason, the eye does not see purely. Our eyes would see differently in the world of material existence if they did not contain remnants from earlier levels of existence. The same is true of our hearing and other senses, which are all contaminated by the desire to see, hear, taste, or otherwise perceive specific things. The so-called desire remaining from earlier incarnations creeps into everything our senses encounter in this incarnation.

The Buddha said that without this desire from earlier incarnations, we would behold the world like divine beings, taking it in without desiring or coveting anything that is not freely offered to us. Our knowledge would not exceed what the di-

vine powers grant us. We would not distinguish between ourselves and the outer world but would experience ourselves as
members of that world. We experience ourselves as separate
from the rest of the world only because we desire something
more than, or different from, the enjoyments that the rest of
the world freely offers us. This desire awakens our awareness
of being different. If we were content with the world as it is,
we would not distinguish ourselves from it. We would experience it as an extension of our own existence. We would never
experience so-called contact with the outer world; we would
not be separate from it, so we couldn't "contact" it. Contact
with the outer world developed gradually as our six organs
developed. Contact triggered what we call sensation, and sensation in turn caused us to cling to the outer world. Clinging
to the outer world, however, causes pain, suffering, worry, and
sorrow.

This is how the Buddha described the inner human being
who causes pain and suffering, sorrow and worry in our world.
His is a sensitive, exalted theory, but it springs directly from
life because an "enlightened one" sensed it as a profound truth
about contemporary human beings. When he became the
Buddha, this bodhisattva, who had spent thousands of years
guiding humanity toward the doctrine of compassion and love,
discovered the true nature and cause of suffering in contemporary human beings. He saw the cause of suffering and explained it to his closest pupils.

The famous sermon at Benares that launched his activity
as the Buddha summed up his experience of the essential ker-
nel of contemporary human existence. He preached a popu-
lar form of what he had conveyed to his pupils in a more
intimate setting, saying that if we recognize the causes of hu-

man existence, we know that life must include suffering and pain. His first lesson was the lesson of suffering in the world. The second is the doctrine of the causes of suffering. Suffering is caused by the desire or thirst for existence, the stealthy remnants of earlier incarnations. Thirsting for existence is the cause of suffering. The third lesson is how to eliminate suffering from the world. Of course suffering can be eliminated by eliminating its cause, that is, by extinguishing the thirst for existence that results from ignorance. The Buddha said that we have abandoned ancient clairvoyant knowledge for a state of ignorance that hides the spiritual world from us. Ignorance is to blame for the thirst for existence, which in turn causes suffering and pain, worry and sorrow. To eliminate these misfortunes from the world, the thirst for existence must disappear. The old knowledge has vanished, and people can no longer use their etheric organs. We can acquire new knowledge, however, through total immersion in what the astral body's deepest forces can supply with the help of physical sense perceptions. The gift of knowledge is acquired only through astral observation, which places demands on the physical body but cannot be developed through physical disciplines. This is approximately what the Buddha said in his first great public speech.

He knew that he had to communicate the knowledge that can be achieved by developing the astral body's forces to the utmost through mighty meditative effort. Knowledge thus achieved is appropriate to the present human condition and has nothing to do with influences from earlier incarnations. The Buddha offered knowledge that had nothing to do with the darkness and ignorance of *samskara*, which slumbers in the human soul. He wanted to exemplify the knowledge that can be acquired by awakening all the astral body's forces in a single incarnation.

The Buddha said suffering in the world is caused by human ignorance of a remnant that persists from earlier incarnations. This remnant causes the ignorance prevalent in the world; it also causes human suffering and pain, worry and sorrow. But when we become aware of our astral forces, we can choose to acquire knowledge that does not depend on anything in the past.

This is the knowledge the great Buddha attempted to convey in the so-called eightfold path. Contemporary individuals who develop the forces he presents in this path achieve knowledge that is not influenced by repeated rebirth. The Buddha himself raised his soul to the highest level accessible to the astral body's strongest forces. In the eightfold path, he wanted to show humankind the route to knowledge uninfluenced by *samskara*. He said that we achieve this type of knowledge by acquiring right views that have nothing to do with sympathy, antipathy, or personal bias. We develop such views purely on the basis of what is presented to us from outside, that is, on the basis of the object's own forces. "Right views," or "right understanding" of issues, is the first step on the eightfold path.

As a second step, we must become independent of persistent remnants of previous incarnations. We must attempt to form judgments based on right views rather than on any other influences. "Right judgment" is the second step.

The third is to express our right views and right judgments correctly when we convey them to the world. We refrain from introducing anything other than our right views into our words and any other expressions of our human nature. This is the "right speech" of Buddhism.

The fourth necessary step is to carry out actions uninfluenced by our sympathies and antipathies, free of the dark rum-
blings of samskara. We permit only our right views, right
judgment, and right speech to affect our deeds. This is "right
action."

The fifth step toward inner liberation is achieving our
proper place in the world. What did the Buddha mean by this?
Many people are unsatisfied with their task in the world and
think they would be better off in a different position. We need
to learn, however, to make the best of the situation that is ours
through birth or destiny. When we are not content with our
station in life, it does not provide the strength we need for
appropriate action in the world. The Buddha called this fifth
step acquiring the "right standpoint."[2]

The sixth step is to make a habit of everything we have
acquired through right views, right judgment, and so forth.
Already as children, we begin to develop specific habits and
inclinations. We must make an effort, however, to give up habits that come from *samskara* and to gradually acquire ones that
result from right views, right judgment, right speech, and so
forth. These are "right habits."

The seventh step is to order our life by not forgetting yesterday when we act today. If we had to learn all our skills anew
each time we attempted to do something, we would never accomplish anything. We must always attempt to recollect or
remember all aspects of our existence, to evaluate what we have
already learned and link the present to the past. This "right
memory" must be acquired on the eightfold path of Buddhism.

The eighth step is accomplished by allowing neither our
preference for a specific opinion nor anything that persists
from previous incarnations to interfere with the purity of our

contemplation of the objects and events we encounter. We allow the objects and events themselves to speak for themselves. This is "right contemplation."

This is the eightfold path of Buddhism. The Buddha told his disciples that following this path would gradually extinguish the thirst for existence that causes suffering and liberate human souls from all the enslaving remnants of past lives. The description of this path gives us a sense of the spirit and origin of Buddhism. We also recognize the importance of the fact that the bodhisattva became a buddha. We know that throughout human evolution, the bodhisattva always worked to give humankind the faculties related to his mission. In ancient times, before the Buddha walked the earth, human beings were dependent on influences flowing into them from the spiritual worlds. We could not use our inner forces to spontaneously produce right speech or right judgment. Because the bodhisattva was responsible for the flow of moral spiritual influences, it was a unique event when he became the Buddha and taught people what he had previously accomplished on their behalf. The human body he produced independently developed forces that had previously come only from above. The body of Gautama Buddha was the first human body of this type. As a result, forces that for epochs had streamed down from spiritual heights existed independently on earth. This accomplishment is of great and far-reaching importance for earthly evolution, because these forces are now accessible to all human beings. The ability to develop the forces of the eightfold path independently and internally, making them the common possession of all human beings, originated in the body of Gautama Buddha. The very fact that the Buddha lived began a process that will eventually enable all of humankind to accomplish the steps of the eightfold path. The Buddha gave human beings the spiritual nourishment he himself had internalized.

In general, such events are not examined by today's material science. Instead, they are often recounted by childlike legends and fairy tales. I have emphasized repeatedly and in many different contexts that fairy tales and legends are often wiser and more scientific than our objective scholarship. Human souls have always sensed a very special truth in the presence of a being such as a bodhisattva, namely, that a quality they would eventually internalize and radiate back into cosmic space initially streamed into them from above. Those dimly capable of perceiving such facts knew that just as the sun's rays shine in the heavens, the strength of the bodhisattva irradiated the earth with the forces of the doctrine of compassion and love. They knew that when the bodhisattva incarnated fully in a human body, he bestowed on human beings a possession that had once been his alone. This gift is now alive in humankind and radiates back into cosmic space just as moonlight reflects the rays of the sun. People have always sensed the exceptional importance of such phenomena and expressed their truths in the form of fairy tales and legends. In the case of the bodhisattva, a remarkable legend emerged in the areas where he lived, and the great event of his life was clothed in a simple story.

The Buddha was once incarnated as a hare at a time when many different creatures searched for food but went hungry because all the food had been eaten. The plants that the hare ate were not suitable food for meat-eating creatures. The hare, who was actually the Buddha, decided to sacrifice himself as food for a Brahman who was passing by. At that very moment the god Shakra appeared and saw the hare's noble deed. A cleft opened in the mountain and swallowed the hare, and the god took ink and painted the hare's image on the moon. Since that time, the image of the Buddha in the form of the hare can be seen on the moon. (In the West, as you know, we see the image of the "man in the moon" instead of the image of a hare.) A Kalmuck legend tells this story even more succinctly: the hare that lives on the moon is there because when the Buddha sacrificed himself, the spirit of the earth drew the hare's picture on the moon. These legends express the great truth of how the bodhisattva became the Buddha and how the Buddha himself devoted a faculty that had belonged to him alone to serve as nourishment for human beings, so that it can shine from human hearts and irradiate the cosmos.

Seers know that the transition from bodhisattva to buddha signifies a being's final incarnation on earth. In that final incarnation, the being in question incarnates fully into a human body. The Buddha sensed the significance of his final incarnation on earth. It would be wrong to believe, however, that such a being withdraws totally from earthly existence when he no longer appears in a physical body. He continues to influence life on earth by assuming a body of a different sort. After his final physical incarnation, he works through a body that may be either astral or etheric in nature.

Such a being, who no longer descends into a physical body but still possesses an astral body, can pervade an ordinary human being who has a physical body, an ether body, an astral body, and an I. The higher being then acts through that person, who becomes an important personality through the activity of forces belonging to a being whose final earthly incarnation has been completed. Thus an astral being unites with the astral member of a human being on earth. How this union occurs can be very complicated. When the Buddha appeared to the shepherds in the image of the "heavenly hosts," he was present not in a physical body, but in an astral body through which he continued to influence the earth.

We distinguish three types of bodies that a buddha can assume. The first is the pre-buddha body through which a bodhisattva works from above. This body maintains contact with the heights and is associated with a bodhisattva mission prior to its transformation into a buddha mission. Hence this body, the Dharmakaya, does not include everything through which such a being acts. The second body, the Sambhogakaya or "body of perfection," fully manifests all the attributes of a bodhisattva in a physical body. The third body is assumed after a bodhisattva achieves enlightenment as a buddha and he works down on the earth as described above. This body is called a Nirmanakaya.

We can say, therefore, that the Buddha's Nirmanakaya, in the form of the angelic hosts, appeared to the shepherds. The Buddha's radiance streamed into the Nirmanakaya that was revealed to the shepherds. After this appearance, however, the Buddha continued to seek ways of influencing events taking place in Palestine at this very important time.

In order to understand the Buddha's ongoing influence, we must briefly recall what anthroposophical lectures have taught us about the nature of the human being. We know that spiritual science distinguishes between several types of birth. In physical birth, an individual sheds the mother's physical covering, as it were. The mother's etheric covering, which surrounds the child until the second dentition just as her physical body surrounds the infant until physical birth, is discarded in the seventh year of life. At puberty, which presently occurs in the fourteenth or fifteenth year of life, the astral covering is discarded. Thus a person's ether body is born as an independent body in the outer world only around age six, and the astral body is born only at puberty when the maternal astral covering is shed.

Let's look at the astral covering that is discarded at puberty. In Palestine when the events we are describing took place, puberty typically began earlier — during the twelfth year of life, under normal circumstances. That was when the mother's astral covering was discarded. Ordinarily, this covering is shed and surrendered to the outer astral world. In the case of the child who was descended from the priestly branch of the house of David, something else happened. In his twelfth year of life, the discarded maternal astral body did not dissolve into the general astral world. Instead, this astral covering, which had protected the young boy from the second dentition to puberty, merged, together with all the enlivening forces that had streamed into it during that period, with the Buddha's descending Nirmanakaya, which had appeared as the heavenly host. The Buddha's Nirmanakaya, which had hovered over and illuminated the child Jesus since his birth, united with the astral covering discarded by the boy Jesus, thus absorbing all the forces that maintain youth in the period between the second dentition and puberty. This rejuvenation made it possible for the Buddha's earlier gift to the world to reappear in the childlike simplicity of the boy Jesus. It enabled the boy to talk in a childlike way about the exalted doctrines of compassion and love that we described today in all their complexity. At his visit to the Temple, those around him were astonished at how he spoke (Luke 2:44-50). This unprecedented ability was due to the Buddha's Nirmanakaya, which surrounded the boy and was rejuvenated, as if in a fountain of youth, by the maternal astral covering he discarded.

Spiritual researchers are aware of this mystery that the author of the Luke Gospel wove into the transformation of the twelve-year-old Jesus in the Temple. Thus the Luke Gospel teaches a form of Buddhism that is accessible to simple, childlike minds. This transformation explains why the boy suddenly spoke differently. His previous manner of speaking was like that of King Kanishka in India, who around that same time called a synod and proclaimed the orthodoxy of ancient Buddhism. The Buddha himself had advanced in the interim, however. He had absorbed the forces of the maternal astral sheath of the child Jesus, which enabled him to speak to human hearts and minds in a new way. Thus the Luke Gospel contains a new Buddhism, rejuvenated as if in a fountain of youth, and states the religion of compassion and love in a way that is easily understandable to the simplest hearts and minds. This mystery is there for us to read, woven into the account of Jesus' life by the author of the Luke Gospel.

Today I had time to describe only part of what actually happened in this scene in the Temple. Subsequent lectures will further illuminate the background of this mystery and clarify earlier and later events in the life of Jesus of Nazareth.

BASEL, SEPTEMBER 17, 1909

NOTES

1. Steiner uses the Hindu/Buddhist term *manas*, both here and in Lecture 5, to mean a faculty of perception related to the physical world. In other works, such as his *Theosophy* (1904), he uses manas differently as "spirit-self": a stage in the higher development of the Self. —*Ed.*

2. This step is usually called "right livelihood" and interpreted more narrowly, referring more specifically to vocation. Books on Buddhism also describe several of the other steps differently — what Steiner calls "right judgment" is often "right aim, or motives," his "right habits" is "right effort," his "right memory" is "right mindfulness, or thoughts." —*Trans.*

FOUR

Formation of the Nathan-Jesus Child

IN THE NEXT FEW DAYS, as we continue to investigate the facts underlying the Luke Gospel, we will find that they become increasingly elusive and intricate. For this reason, please keep in mind that the lectures are cumulative; the content of each lecture builds upon the last. It will prove impossible to understand an individual lecture or lectures without considering the context supplied by other lectures. Because this is especially true of today's lecture and tomorrow's, please refrain until tomorrow from asking how their content relates to other lecture cycles that touched on the same subject.

We closed yesterday with the statement that the Buddha's Nirmanakaya was revealed in our world during what the Luke Gospel describes as the annunciation to the shepherds. We said that the rejuvenated Buddhist worldview flowed into the world through Christianity when the maternal astral body separated from the adolescent Jesus and was absorbed by the Buddha's Nirmanakaya. From that moment, a specific being united the Buddha's Nirmanakaya, or spirit body, and the maternal astral body that surrounded the boy Jesus until age twelve.

This fact raises the following issue. Ordinarily, when the maternal astral body separates from a growing human being and the young person's own astral body is born, the maternal astral body dissolves into the general astral world. In our current evolutionary cycle, the maternal astrality surrounding an ordinary human being could not possibly receive a being as exalted as the Buddha's Nirmanakaya, so there must have been something special about the astral covering discarded by the boy Jesus that allowed it to undergo the union that rejuvenated Buddhism. In other words, a very special being must have incarnated into the body of the boy Jesus so that rejuvenating forces radiated into his maternal astral covering during the first twelve years of his life. The being who lived and grew in the boy Jesus from birth to age twelve was no ordinary human being but a very special being capable of radiating forces of rejuvenation into the covering that was to be discarded.

To gain an idea of how it is possible for a child to affect his suprasensible coverings in such an unusual way, we can initially approach this phenomenon only through a comparison that serves to illustrate what actually happened. Individual forces that are present only as potentials in the embryo and the newborn gradually appear in the course of a normal human life. The child grows, both physically and spiritually, and soul forces unfold gradually. You can read about this process in my booklet *The Education of the Child in the Light of Spiritual Science.*[1] Try to imagine the gradual internal development of emotional and intellectual forces. At ages seven, fourteen, and twenty-one, forces appear that were previously absent — or present to a lesser extent. Imagine what happens in the normal course of a human life, and then imagine that we experimentally alter the normal, average course of development. Suppose, for example, that we do not permit this child to take in what others normally learn between the ages of twelve and eighteen in the ordinary way. Instead, we provide an artificial opportunity for the child to learn with a freshness that preserves the soul's creative influence. If we want to artificially induce exceptional productivity, we cannot allow the child to grow up in the usual way. Let me emphasize that this experiment is purely hypothetical and not intended for actual implementation. I am simply using it as an example, not recommending it as an educational model.

We attempt to raise this individual to be an exceptionally inventive spirit, someone who not only enlivens the human capacity for thinking but also achieves a high level of creativity and productivity later in life. Above all else, we must prevent our experimental subject from learning the way other children learn, beginning around age six. This child must learn as little as possible about the usual academic subjects and must be allowed to go on playing until around age ten. He may not be able to add at age nine and may still read poorly at age eight. Such treatment allows an individual's forces to develop very differently; the soul handles what it is taught very differently. In such a child, the childlike forces that are suppressed by ordinary instruction are preserved until around age ten and are then used to understand what is taught in a very different way, making the individual's faculties especially productive. When a child is allowed to remain childlike for as long as possible, the astral covering released at puberty possesses unusually fresh, youthful forces that can be perceived by clairvoyants. Such an astral covering could indeed be used by a being such as the Buddha's Nirmanakaya. This experiment would not only extend childhood but would also imbue the maternal astral covering with specific childlike or youthful forces that can then be reused to nourish and rejuvenate a being descending from spiritual heights.

I do not mean to suggest that this experiment should actually be implemented. It is not a suitable model for modern education. Today we must leave certain things to the gods, so to speak, because the gods can implement them safely while human beings cannot. Occasionally, however, you hear about an individual who seemed untalented as a child and was thought to be stupid for years and years until he or she suddenly "caught on" and proceeded to accomplish highly creative work in a specific field. In such cases, the gods are experimenting. They allow such individuals to remain childlike for longer than normal and make them capable of learning only later in life. In particular, the gods experiment with children who seem alert and quick to understand but have no interest in learning when they enter school.

Something similar must have happened — and in fact did happen, but to an infinitely greater extent — to the boy Jesus who was to provide the Buddha's Nirmanakaya with its rejuvenating mantle of maternal astrality. Such mysterious facts, which individuals may freely accept or reject, can be confirmed by anthroposophists who are prepared to receive them. If you approach these mysterious facts in the right way and are not overhasty in judging them, you will find that they are confirmed by material facts on the physical plane and by the contents of the Gospels or historical records. If the sources of occultists are correct, their statements — that is, the facts they derive from higher worlds and pass on to the rest of humankind — will withstand precise scrutiny. If we apply appropriate tests, we will always find such statements confirmed by what we learn in the physical world from written documents or from science.

Thus the parents described in the Luke Gospel must have given birth to a highly exceptional child endowed from birth with especially strong youthful or childlike forces that remained fresh and healthy in all respects as the boy grew up. This is what must have happened. Under normal circumstances, no child and no parents would have possessed the necessary forces. Under the normal circumstances prevailing among human beings of those times, it would have been impossible to find either the individuality or the parents to support such an incarnation. We must recall what our anthroposophical experience has taught us if we want to understand the very special possibilities that allowed such an incarnation to happen.

We know that modern human beings evolved from the primeval human race of ancient Atlantis, which evolved in turn from the ancient Lemurians. Spiritual science discloses facts about the evolution of humankind that are very different from the facts of material science, which are based exclusively on sensory perception. Prior to our own cultural epoch, humankind passed through the Greco-Latin stage of cultural development, which was preceded by the Egypto-Chaldean, ancient Persian, and ancient Indian cultures. Earlier still, spiritual research reveals a great catastrophe that changed the entire face of the earth. Before this cataclysmic event, the extensive continent known as ancient Atlantis occupied the area that is now the Atlantic Ocean, and most of the area now inhabited by Europeans, Asians, and Africans was under water. The great Atlantean upheaval of the earth's watery element changed the face of the earth. Before this catastrophe, most human beings lived on the Atlantean continent. As I have often described, these people were different from modern human beings. Their great clairvoyant leaders and priests foresaw the approach of the great catastrophe and guided people away from Atlantis. Most Atlanteans moved east, but some moved west and became the ancestors of native American populations. Thus we must see the ancient Atlanteans as the forebears of modern humankind. The Atlanteans in turn were descended from earlier humans who looked quite different and inhabited the continent of ancient Lemuria, which was located in the area now surrounded by Asia, Africa, and Australia. Since the details can be found in my book *An Outline of Esoteric Science*, I will mention only the aspects that are essential to today's discussion.[2]

The Akashic record of very ancient times provides wonderful evidence that supports what we find in the Bible and other religious documents and enables us to understand these documents correctly. For example, biblical accounts of a single human couple, Adam and Eve, supposedly the ancestors of all humanity, have been questioned by materialistic science. Especially around the middle of the nineteenth century, this issue stimulated a great deal of scientific debate.

To summarize what the Akashic record tells us, the earth has a long prehistory. Even the Lemurian epoch was not the earth's first manifestation. Our present Earth is the re-embodiment of earlier planetary stages — old Moon, old Sun, and old Saturn. Furthermore, we know that the task of the earth's gradual evolution is to add the I, the fourth member of the human constitution, to the three bodies that gradually evolved during earlier embodiments of the earth — the physical body on Saturn, the ether body on the Sun, and the astral body on the Moon. All the times that preceded the Lemurian epoch served simply to prepare for the earth's mission. In Lemurian times, the human being first assumed a form that was capable of developing the fourth member, the I. A seminal I began to develop in the three members that the human being had gradually acquired. Thus we can say that changes on earth allowed the human being to become the bearer of an I. Even prior to Lemurian times, the earth was populated by human beings, but they were very different from modern humans. They did not incorporate the I and possessed only the physical, etheric, and astral bodies that they had acquired during the Saturn, Sun, and Moon stages.

The Akashic record also tells us about the cosmic events that allowed human beings to mature to this point. We know that at the beginning of its present evolutionary stage, Earth was united with the Sun and Moon. The Sun then separated from this cosmic mass, leaving behind a planetary body that combined our present Earth and Moon. We also know, however, that if Earth had remained united with the Moon, human beings would have mummified. The hardening of the human form was prevented by evicting the beings and substances belonging to the Moon. Only after the Moon's separation were human beings able to assume their present form and to become bearers of the I. This process did not happen all at once, however. The Sun separated gradually from Earth, and even after that, human evolution could not progress as long as the Moon remained part of Earth. Physical matter became increasingly dense, and human bodies slowly hardened. The human souls of that time existed on a lower level than they do now but were already passing through successive incarnations or embodiments, leaving material embodiment to pass through a spiritual world and then reappearing in a new embodiment. But before the Moon's separation from Earth, certain circumstances presented obstacles to Earth's continued evolution. Some disembodied human souls that had entered the spiritual world and were attempting to reincarnate encountered physical bodies that had become too hard to receive incarnating souls. For a time, souls wanting to return to Earth could not reincarnate because they found no suitable earthly bodies. Only the strongest souls were able to subdue the hardened physical substance they encountered and incarnate successfully on Earth. All others could not descend into bodies and had to return to the spiritual world. This situation was typical of the time before the Moon's separation. Ever fewer strong souls were able to subdue matter and populate the earth, and there were fewer and fewer human beings on Earth because incarnating souls found no suitable bodies.

What happened to the souls who could not find bodies? They were transported to the other planets that had formed from the common cosmic mass. Some souls were transported to Saturn, others to Jupiter, Mars, Venus, or Mercury. There was a long wintry period on Earth when only the strongest souls incarnated there. The weaker souls, meanwhile, were placed in the care of the other planets in our solar system.

At a specific point in the Lemurian epoch, it was indeed

true — or at least almost true — that only one human couple remained strong enough to subdue recalcitrant human substance and could therefore continue to incarnate throughout the entire Earth embodiment of our planet. At that time, however, the Moon separated from Earth, allowing human substance to become more refined and suitable for weaker human souls. Thus descendants of this single ancestral human couple were able to incarnate into substance that was softer than what had existed before the Moon's separation. Gradually all the souls that had been transported to Mars, Jupiter, Venus, and so on returned to Earth. As the descendants of the ancestral couple multiplied, souls gradually repopulated the earth. The time from the end of the Lemurian period until well into the Atlantean period saw the return of increasing numbers of souls who had been waiting on other planets until they could once again reincarnate in earthly bodies. These souls constituted the population of Atlantis.

The Atlanteans were led by the initiates of the Atlantean oracles, great centers of guidance on the continent of Atlantis. Some were called Mars oracles, others Jupiter or Saturn oracles, and so forth. The Mars oracles provided instruction and leadership for human souls who had spent the waiting period on Mars, while the Jupiter oracles ministered to those who had been on Jupiter, and so forth. During Atlantean times, the great central oracle of the Sun educated only the few individuals most closely descended from the single ancestral couple that had survived the great crisis on Earth. The Bible calls these two people Adam and Eve. Thus the Akashic record confirms seemingly improbable biblical accounts. The great oracle that was known as the Sun oracle supervised all the others and was headed by the greatest Atlantean Sun initiate,

Manu, who was also the leader of the Atlantean population. As the Atlantean catastrophe approached, his task was to assemble the people he found most suitable and move with them to the east, where he established a settlement that served as the source of post-Atlantean culture. He chose his associates from among the direct descendants of Adam and Eve, the ancestral souls who had survived the winter of the earth. Manu's chosen students lived in close proximity to the great initiate of the Sun oracle, and care and attention were lavished upon them. The purpose of their instruction was to allow the right influences to flow from Manu's initiation center at all times in humankind's evolution.

At certain points in time, cultures must be rejuvenated. Old traditions require a new impetus to provide human culture with a new element. This was the immediate goal of the center led by the Sun initiate, and it could be accomplished in any number of different ways. In the earliest period of post-Atlantean cultural development, this oracle center, whose location in Asia remained a secret, supplied appropriate guidance for different cultures by sending out individuals carefully prepared to meet the needs of the respective ethnic groups.

At a specific time five or six centuries after the appearance of the great Buddha, however, it became necessary to rejuvenate Buddhism. The ancient, mature worldview whose apex had been proclaimed by the great Buddha needed to be immersed in a fountain of youth so that it could reappear in a fresh new form. Humankind needed an influx of specific forces of youth that did not exist in any individuality currently at work on earth.

Beings who work on behalf of the cosmos wear down their forces — that is, they grow old. If we look back in time on the development of one culture after another — first the ancient Indian culture, then the ancient Persian, then the Egypto-Chaldean, and so on — we see that in each epoch, humankind had great and important leaders who sacrificed their best forces for the progress of the human race. The great holy *rishis* sacrificed their best forces, as did Zarathustra, the founder of Persian culture, and Hermes, Moses, and the leaders of Chaldean culture. All sacrificed their best forces. In terms of their influence, they were the best and most appropriate leaders for their times. For example, the soul of a personality incarnated in ancient India reappeared repeatedly, growing older and more mature as it reincarnated in the Persian and Egypto-Chaldean cultures. It acquired increasingly mature forces but lost the fresh forces of youth. Old souls that have worked on themselves through many incarnations accomplish great deeds on behalf of humanity and teach great ideas, but they sacrifice youthful freshness and strength for the sake of this progress.

Let's consider Zarathustra as an example of one of the greatest individualities to influence the course of human evolution. From the depths of the spiritual world, Zarathustra proclaimed the great tidings of the Sun spirit, pointing his contemporaries to the great spirit who would later appear as the Christ. Zarathustra spoke great, significant words about Ahura Mazda, who dwelt in the Sun and would one day come down to Earth. The holy *rishis* had said that this being, whom they called Vishva Karman, existed outside their sphere, but Zarathustra called him Ahura Mazda and proclaimed his significance for human evolution.

The spirit that lived in the Zarathustra body was already tremendously mature when Zarathustra founded the culture of ancient Persia. We can imagine this individuality rising ever higher and becoming older and increasingly mature and capable of greater sacrifices on humanity's behalf in subsequent incarnations. If you attended some of my other lectures, you know that Zarathustra bestowed his astral body on Hermes, the leader of Egyptian culture, and his ether body on Moses, the leader of the Hebrew people. Only the most highly evolved souls are capable of such gifts, and Zarathustra was one such individuality. Six hundred years before Christ, when the Buddha was active in India, the great teacher Nazarathos or Zarathas, who taught Pythagoras, appeared in Chaldea as a later incarnation and further maturation of the great soul who led and inaugurated Persian culture.

As you will see from all this, however, this soul could not rejuvenate Buddhism. Because he had achieved such great heights in the course of his incarnations, the Zarathustra being could not possibly contribute the fresh, youthful forces that typically develop before the onset of puberty. If this being had incarnated as a child at the beginning of the Christian era, that child would not have been able to develop in ways that could support the events that had become necessary.

If we look at the developmental stages of all the individualities of that time, we find no one who could be born with the ability to contribute the fresh, youthful forces needed to rejuvenate Buddhism. We have just considered the uniquely great Zarathustra individuality as an example, and even he would have been unable to suitably enliven the body of Jesus until the envelope of maternal astrality was discarded and merged with the Buddha's Nirmanakaya.

Where, then, was the great enlivening power of the Jesus body to come from? It came from the great mother lodge of humanity, led by the great Sun initiate Manu. A great individual force, lavished with care and attention in the great mother lodge, was sent down into the child who was born to the couple the Luke Gospel calls Joseph and Mary. This child received the best and strongest of the individualities fostered by the Sun oracle.

To discover who this individuality was, we must go back to a time that predates Lucifer's influence on the human astral body. Luciferic beings began to influence humanity when the earth was populated by the single couple who were the forebears of all subsequently incarnating human beings. These two individuals were strong enough to conquer human substance so that they could incarnate, but they were not strong enough to resist Lucifer's influence, which entered their astral bodies. As a result of this influence, it was not possible for all of Adam and Eve's forces to be transmitted to their blood descendants. Physical bodies had to reproduce down through the generations, but the guiding powers of humankind sequestered an aspect of the ether body. The Bible expresses this by saying that human beings, having eaten of the tree of the knowledge of good and evil — that is, having tasted the consequences of the Luciferic influence — had to be prevented from eating the fruit of the tree of life. This means that a certain portion of the ether body's forces were retained and not transmitted to Adam and Eve's descendants. Some of Adam's forces were taken from him after the Fall, and this innocent part of Adam was preserved in the great mother lodge of humanity, where care and attention were lavished upon it. This aspect of Adam's soul had not been involved in events leading up to the Fall and was therefore untouched by human guilt. In it, the original forces of the Adam individuality were preserved. They were later guided into the child who was born to Joseph and Mary. During the first years of Jesus' life, the forces of the original ancestral father of humanity served as his "provisional I."

This soul had certainly remained very young. It had undergone different incarnations but was kept at a much earlier level of development, just as we artificially attempted to hold back the child in our hypothetical educational experiment. In the infant son born to Joseph and Mary, the ancestral father of humanity, the "old Adam," came to life as a "new Adam." Paul was aware of this fact, which lies hidden behind the words of 1 Corinthians 15:45.[3] The Evangelist Luke, as one of Paul's students, was also aware of it, and his knowledge accounts for a rather strange turn of phrase. He knew that something special was needed to guide this spiritual substance into humankind, and that a direct blood relationship to Adam was required. This is why Luke lists Joseph's ancestry all the way back to Adam, who emerged directly from the spiritual world, and speaks of Adam as the "son of God." In the Luke Gospel, the sequence of generations leads back to God (Luke 3:23-38).

These verses listing the ancestors of Jesus conceal a significant mystery, namely, that common blood must flow through the generations in an uninterrupted sequence to the last descendant so that when the allotted time has passed the spirit, too, can be guided into the last descendant. Thus the body that was born to Joseph and Mary received an infinitely youthful spirit untouched by earthly destiny, a young soul whose forces originated in ancient Lemuria. Only this spirit was strong enough flow out completely into the maternal astral body, imbuing it with the forces it needed to merge fruitfully with the Buddha's Nirmanakaya.

How, then, does the Luke Gospel describe Jesus of Nazareth? It first describes a human being whose blood ancestry, the line of descent of the physical body, reaches back to Adam, to the time when human life on the depopulated Earth was saved by a single ancestral couple. It goes on to describe, from the perspective of reincarnation, the reembodiment of the human soul that waited the longest to reincarnate. The Adam soul that existed before the Fall appears again in the boy Jesus. As fantastical as it may sound to modern humanity, we know that the individuality guided by the great mother lodge of humanity into the infant Jesus was not only descended from the physically oldest generation of humans but was also the reembodiment of the first human being. Now we can identify the being who was presented to Simeon in the temple. When Luke called this being the "son of God," he was not speaking about the present human body. He was testifying that this being was the reincarnation of the oldest ancestor of the human race.

Let me summarize all this briefly. Five or six centuries before the beginning of the Christian era, a great bodhisattva lived in India. His mission was to bring truths to humankind, to provide the stimulus for truths that would eventually emerge from within human beings. By fulfilling his mission, he became the Buddha and no longer needed to incarnate into an earthly body corresponding completely to his individuality. He reappeared, however, in the Nirmanakaya, the body of transformations, descending only as far as the etheric and astral worlds. The shepherds, momentarily clairvoyant, saw this being in the form of the angelic hosts who accompanied the proclamation to the shepherds. With good reason, this being inclined toward the child who was born to Joseph and Mary.

Of necessity, the great Buddha's gift to humankind had appeared in a mature form. This gift was difficult to understand; it existed on an exalted level of spiritual meaning. To make it bear fruit for all of humankind, a fresh new force of youth had to flow into what the Buddha had accomplished. The Buddha had imbibed this force out of the earth by inclining over the human child from whom he would later receive all the youthful forces of a disintegrating maternal astral body. The Buddha was more aware than anyone else that this infant's physical body could be traced back to the ancestral father of all humankind, and his soul to the soul — both old and young — of humankind during the Lemurian epoch. The Buddha recognized the child as the incarnation of the new Adam, as the mother-soul of all humanity, which remained young throughout the epochs. The fresh forces of the child's life radiated into the astral body that was released at puberty and rose to merge with the Buddha's Nirmanakaya.

These are only some of the facts that allow us to understand the wonderful mystery of Palestine. Now we can identify the being who was born in Bethlehem after Joseph and Mary traveled there from Nazareth. We know whose coming was announced to the shepherds. This, however, is only one aspect of the story. The beginning of the Christian era was full of strange and significant happenings leading to the greatest event in humankind's evolution. We must consider other aspects in order to understand what gradually led to this great event.

Among the ancient Hebrews, all those "of the house and lineage of David" were descended from a common ancestor, David. The Bible tells us that David had two sons, Solomon and Nathan (2 Sam. 5:14). Two lines of descent, the Solomonic line and the Nathanic line, counted David as their common ancestor. Ignoring the intermediary links, we can say that descendants of both the Solomonic and Nathanic lines lived in Palestine at the beginning of our era. One descendant of the Nathanic branch of the house of David was a man named Joseph, a native of Nazareth. His wife's name was Mary. Surprisingly enough, a native of Bethlehem descended from the Solomonic branch was also named Joseph, and he too was married to a woman named Mary. Thus at the beginning of the Christian era there were two couples named Joseph and Mary living in Palestine. One couple was descended from the Solomonic branch of the house of David, that is, from the kingly lineage, while the other couple in Nazareth were descendants of the Nathanic or priestly branch. The child I described yesterday and today, the child who supplied the maternal astral body that was absorbed into the Buddha's Nirmanakaya, was born to the couple of Nathanic descent. As that child's birth approached, his parents, the Nathanic couple, left Nazareth to go to Bethlehem "to be enrolled," as Luke says (Luke 2:4-5).

The other couple, not originally from Nazareth — we must take the Gospels literally — lived in Bethlehem as described by the author of the Matthew Gospel (Matthew 2:1). The Gospels always tell the truth; there are no conundrums to be solved. Through anthroposophy, people will again begin to take the Gospels literally. A son, also named Jesus, was born to this Solomonic couple, and his body also supported the incarnation of a mighty individuality. The task of this child — so profound is the wisdom of the cosmos — was not to supply a maternal astral body with fresh, youthful forces but rather to bestow the gifts of a mature soul on humankind. All of the relevant forces guided this child to become the incarnation of the individuality who once taught about Ahura Mazda in Persia, the individuality who gave his astral body to Hermes and his ether body to Moses. This being, who reappeared as Zarathas or Nazarathos, the great Chaldean teacher of Pythagoras, is none other than the Zarathustra individuality. The I-being of Zarathustra was reincarnated in the child who was born, as the Matthew Gospel tells us, to a couple named Joseph and Mary, natives of Bethlehem who belonged to the kingly or Solomonic branch of the house of David.

As you see, we find part of the truth in Matthew and the other part in Luke. We must take them both literally, because the truth of the cosmos is complicated. Now we can identify the individuality who was born into the priestly branch of the house of David, but we also know that the individuality once active in Persia as Zarathustra, the founder of the royal magic of Persia, was born into the kingly branch. Thus these two individualities led parallel lives — the young Adam individuality in the child belonging to the priestly branch of the house of David, and the Zarathustra individuality in the child of kingly descent.

Tomorrow we will learn more about how and why this all happened and about further events in Palestine.

BASEL, SEPTEMBER 18, 1909

NOTES

1. Rudolf Steiner, *The Education of the Child and Early Lectures on Education.* Hudson, N.Y.: Anthroposophic Press, 1996. (GA 34, first published in 1907 in the magazine *Luzifer-Gnosis.*)

2. Rudolf Steiner, *An Outline of Esoteric Science.* Hudson, N.Y.: Anthroposophic Press, 1997.

3. 1 Corinthians 15:45: "Thus it is written, The first man Adam became a living being, and the last Adam became a quickening spirit."

FIVE

Contributions to the Nathan Jesus from Buddha and Zarathustra

Each of the great spiritual currents coursing through the human world has its own particular mission. These currents do not always appear singly. They are separated during certain epochs, but at other times they intersect and fructify each other in a great variety of ways. The event in Palestine in particular represents a great and mighty confluence of spiritual currents, and our task here is to call this event to mind with increasing clarity. Worldviews, however, do not move as abstractly as we might imagine, passing through the air to unite in a point. They move through beings, through individualities. To appear in the first place, a worldview must be carried by an individuality, and when spiritual currents mingle and fructify each other, something exceptional must take place in their carriers.

The concrete meeting of the two great spiritual currents of Buddhism and Zoroastrianism in the event in Palestine, as described in yesterday's lecture, may have seemed very complex. If we only had to speak abstractly rather than to deal with concrete events, we would only have to demonstrate how the two worldviews as such came together. As anthroposophists, however, we must leave the realm of the abstract and become increasingly concrete, and thus our task is to identify not only the content of such worldviews but also the individualities who carry them. It should not surprise you that such a great and mighty event as the confluence of Buddhism and Zoroastrianism produced very complicated external situations and required slow, gradual preparation.

As we saw, Buddhism pervaded the child described in the Luke Gospel, the son of Joseph and Mary of Nazareth, who were descended from the Nathanic branch of the house of David. Buddhism worked through this personality. In contrast, we saw the child Jesus described by the Matthew Gospel, the child of Joseph and Mary of Bethlehem, who were descended from the Solomonic branch of the house of David. This second boy Jesus received the I-being of Zarathustra, the founder of ancient Persian culture. Thus at the beginning of our era, the Luke and Matthew Gospels described how the currents Buddhism and Zoroastrianism respectively manifested in actual individualities. The birth dates of the two boys did not coincide exactly.

Today, of course, I will have to tell you something that you will not find in the Gospels. The Akashic record chronicles events whose effects and consequences are described in the Gospels, although the Evangelists could not report the events themselves. You will understand the Gospel accounts better by learning what the Akashic record reveals about them. We must keep in mind that what John says at the end of his Gospel, that "the world itself could not contain the books that would be written" (John 21:25), is true of all the Gospels. Christianity's revelations to humankind were not accomplished once and for all, written down and presented to the world in their entirety in book form. There is truth in the saying, "I am with you always, even unto the end of the world" (Matt. 28:20). Christ is not dead; he is with us as a living being. If our spiritual eyes are open, we can always receive what he offers us. Christianity is a living spiritual current and its revelations will endure as long as human beings are able to receive them. Today, therefore, I will mention certain facts that you will not find in the Gospels, although their consequences are described there. These facts can be checked against the facts of the physical world, which will confirm them.

The births of the two Jesus children were separated by several months. Both the Jesus of the Luke Gospel and John the Baptist were born late enough to avoid the slaughter of the innocents in Bethlehem. Have you ever read about this slaughter and wondered how John survived? The Jesus of the Matthew Gospel was taken to Egypt by his parents, and John was born at the same time or slightly earlier but is said to have remained in Palestine, where he should have died in Herod's murderous rampage. You see, matters like this require careful thought. If in fact all children under the age of two years were killed, John should have died too. The apparently contradictory accounts in the Gospels make sense once you become aware of the facts of the Akashic record. You realize that the events described in the Matthew and Luke Gospels did not happen at the same time and that both John and the Nathanic

Jesus were born after the slaughter of the innocents in Bethlehem. The difference in timing was only a matter of months, but it was enough to guarantee their survival. The hidden facts of the Akashic record will also help you understand the Jesus of the Matthew Gospel. The individuality we know as the Zarathustra of ancient Persian culture reincarnated in this boy. We know that Zarathustra gave the Persians the great religion of Ahura Mazda, the great Sun-being. We must imagine this Sun-being as the soul-spiritual portion of the entity whose physical portion is the outer, material Sun. Zarathustra said, "Behold not only the radiance of the physical Sun; behold also the mighty being who bestows his benevolent spiritual effects on us just as the physical Sun gives us light and warmth." To the Persians, Zarathustra proclaimed the existence of Ahura Mazda, who would later be called the Christ. In Zarathustra's time, this being did not yet walk the earth. Zarathustra could only point to the Sun, saying, "He lives there and is gradually approaching the earth; one day he will inhabit an earthly body."

Here we see the great and mighty difference between Zoroastrianism and Buddhism. As long as the two were separate, they were profoundly different, but the differences were eliminated when they coincided in, and were rejuvenated by, the event in Palestine.

Let's look once more at the Buddha's gift to the world. We described the Buddha's eightfold path, which human souls must follow in order to escape the negative effects of karma. The Buddha exemplified the qualities of compassion and love that human beings would gradually become able to develop on the basis of personal convictions and morality. I also told you that the moment the bodhisattva being became the Bud-

dha was a unique moment in human evolution. If the bodhisattva had not appeared completely in the body of the great
Gautama Buddha, individual human souls would not have
been able to receive the lawfulness known as *dharma*, which
human beings develop from within only by eliminating the
astral content of their souls in order to free themselves from
all the harmful effects of karma. The Buddha legend points to
this fact in a wonderful way when it says that the Buddha had
succeeded in "setting the wheel of the law rolling." That is, when
the bodhisattva was enlightened and became the Buddha, a
wave flowed over all of humankind, and as a consequence individuals gradually learned to develop *dharma* from within
their own souls and to accomplish the profound changes pre-
scribed in the eightfold path.

Such was the task of this bodhisattva. Individual tasks are
distributed among great individualities, and in the original
Buddhism we recognize the great ideal of personal, individual
soul experience. The Buddha preached the ideal of the human
soul, of what the human being is and can become. But that
one goal was enough for this individuality. Because Buddhism
is concerned with inwardness and with individual human development, the real, original Buddhism contains no cosmological teachings, although they were incorporated later in a
very understandable attempt to provide an all-encompassing
worldview. The bodhisattva's actual mission, however, was to
present the doctrine of the inwardness of each individual soul.
In fact, in some sermons the Buddha refused to comment on
cosmic relationships. His teachings are all formulated to allow the human souls who receive them to become better and
better. The original Buddhism views the human being as an
independent entity and disregards the great cosmic womb from

which human beings emerged. The warm and inward effect of Buddhism — if correctly perceived — on the human soul is due to the specific nature of the bodhisattva's mission, as is the warmth of feeling we experience in the rejuvenation of the Buddha's teachings in the Luke Gospel.

The individuality who incarnated among the ancient Persians as Zarathustra had a very different, even opposite task. Zarathustra taught people to recognize an external divinity and to comprehend the great cosmos in spiritual terms. In contrast, the Buddha taught people to look inward and said that as human beings practice self-development, ignorance gradually gives way to the "six organs" — that is, to the five sense organs and *manas*. The broader world, however, gives birth to all aspects of the human being. We would not have light-sensitive eyes if the light had not given birth to eyes in the physical body. Goethe says that the eye is created by and for light.[1] This statement contains a profound truth. Light shaped the eyes from previously undifferentiated organs in the human body. Similarly, all the spiritual forces of the cosmos work to develop inner aspects of the human being. Every inner phenomenon therefore corresponds to an outer one. Forces present within the human being initially stream in from outside.

Zarathustra's task was to draw attention to the outer phenomena that surround the human being. For example, Zarathustra talked about the six *amshaspands* or great guardian spirits. (There are actually twelve of them, but the other six are hidden.) The *amshaspands*, whom Zarathustra described as the creators at work behind the human being, shape human organs from outside. Zarathustra identified the great guardian spirits, the creative forces outside us, while the Buddha identified the forces hidden within the human being. But Zarathustra also identified forces and beings subordinate to the *amshaspands*, such as the twenty-eight *izeds* who work on human internal organs from outside. While the Buddha identified the actual thought substance from which thoughts ascend in the human soul, Zarathustra identified the *fravashis*, the creative cosmic thoughts that are distributed throughout the world around us and reflected in human thoughts.

Thus Zarathustra's task was to proclaim a worldview that deciphered and analyzed the outer world, a worldview that would equip people to tackle and transform that world. Zarathustra's mission harmonizes completely with the unique character of the ancient Persians. We might also say that Zarathustra was entrusted with teaching people the strength and competence they needed for activity in the outer world, although some of the consequences may repel modern human beings. His mission was to imbue people with the strength, competence, and certainty needed for outer activity, to support them with the knowledge that they drew strength not only from their own inner nature but also from resting in the womb of a divine spiritual world. His task was to make us realize that wherever we go, we are not alone. We inhabit a cosmos pervaded with spirit; we belong to the cosmic gods and spirits. We are born out of the spirit and rest in the spirit. With every breath we take, we inhale divine spirit; with each exhalation we sacrifice to the great spirit. To correspond to his mission, Zarathustra's initiation had to be very different from that of the other great missionaries to humankind.

Let's recall what the individuality who incarnated as Zarathustra was able to do. He achieved such a high level of development that he was also able to support Egyptian culture, which succeeded the culture of ancient Persia. Zarathustra had two pupils, the individuality who later reappeared as the Egyptian Hermes and the one who later reappeared as Moses. When these two individualities reincarnated to continue their work on behalf of humankind, the astral body that Zarathustra had sacrificed was incorporated into Hermes. We must recognize that Zarathustra's astral body reincarnated in the Egyptian Hermes to allow all the outer science that Zarathustra had absorbed to reappear in the material world. Moses received Zarathustra's ether body. Because everything that develops over time is linked to the ether body, Moses — when he became aware of the mysteries of his ether body — was able to awaken temporal processes in the great and mighty images we encounter in Genesis. Thus the power of Zarathustra's individuality worked on, inaugurating and influencing both the Egyptian and the ancient Hebrew cultures.

The I-being of such an individuality is also destined for further greatness. Zarathustra's I continued to incarnate in different personalities, because a being who learns to give away its original astral and etheric bodies is always able to consecrate another astral body and strengthen another ether body. In ancient Chaldea around six hundred years before the beginning of our era, Zarathustra was reborn as Zarathas or Nazarathos, who became a teacher in the Chaldean mystery center and the teacher of Pythagoras. This personality achieved great and mighty insights into the outer world. If we immerse ourselves in Chaldean wisdom with true understanding by applying anthroposophical rather than anthropological methods, we can sense the importance of what Zarathustra, in the personality of Zarathas, taught in the mystery schools of the ancient Chaldeans.

Everything Zarathustra taught, all his gifts to the world, targeted the outer world and attempted to imbue it with order and harmony. Thus social structures and the art of building and organizing empires in ways that supported human progress were also part of Zarathustra's mission, and it is true that his pupils were not only great magicians or great initiates, but also kings who understood the art of creating outer social structures and social order.

The Chaldean mystery schools developed a great similarity to the individuality — not the personality — of Zarathustra. The wise men of the Orient felt related to their great leader and saw in him humankind's star, for Zoroaster means "golden star" or "shining star." In him they saw the reflected glory of the Sun itself. Their master's reappearance in Bethlehem could not remain hidden from their profound wisdom. Led by their star, they brought him outer tokens of the gifts he had given to human beings. The best that could be given to members of Zarathustra's school was knowledge of the outer world, of the secrets of the cosmos, which the astral body draws into human thinking, feeling, and willing. Zarathustra's students attempted to imbue their soul forces of thinking, feeling, and willing with wisdom drawn from the deepest foundations of the divine spiritual world. This wisdom was symbolized by gold, frankincense, and myrrh: gold for thinking, frankincense for the piety that pervades our feeling, and myrrh for strength of will. The wise men's gifts confirmed their close connection to their master when they reappeared before him at his birth in Bethlehem. The writer of the Matthew Gospel accurately recounts how the wise men influenced by Zarathustra knew that he had reappeared in human form and expressed their relationship to him by offering him gold, frankincense, and myrrh as symbols of the best that he had given them (Matt. 2:11).

In order to reappear in a rejuvenated form and give again all his gifts to humankind, Zarathustra needed to be able to work forcefully through the personality of the Jesus descended from the Solomonic branch of the house of David. This effort required Zarathustra to summon up all the forces he had ever possessed. For this reason, he could not incarnate into a body descended from the priestly branch of the house of David but had to be born into the kingly line of descent. This is why the Matthew Gospel lists King Solomon rather than Nathan the priest as the ancestor of the child who was the reincarnation of Zarathustra. The ancient books of wisdom of the Near East have always pointed to these events. If we understand these books correctly, we read them differently from those who confuse the facts because they do not know what really happened. In the Old Testament, for example, a prophesy in the apocryphal book of Enoch predicts the appearance of a Nathanic Messiah descended from the priestly line, while another prophesy in Psalms predicts a Messiah of kingly lineage. All of the details in the Scriptures coincide with the facts we learn from the Akashic record.

At this point, Zarathustra had to summon up every single power he had ever possessed, but how was he to do so, since he had given the contents of his astral and ether bodies to the Egyptian and ancient Hebrew cultures — that is, to Hermes and Moses, respectively? He had to reunite himself with these forces, to retrieve them from Egypt, as it were. A profound mystery is revealed here: the Jesus of the Solomonic branch of the house of David, who is the reincarnation of Zarathustra, must and does go to Egypt, where he finds the forces that streamed out of the astral and etheric bodies that he once gave to Hermes and Moses. Because he had influenced the culture of Egypt, he had to retrieve the forces he had left there. The "flight to Egypt" occurred so that Zarathustra could reabsorb forces he needed in order to give humankind a rejuvenated form of what he had bestowed on human beings in the past.

Thus we see that Matthew correctly describes the Jesus whose parents came from Bethlehem. Luke alone reports that the parents of his Jesus were from Nazareth and that Jesus was born during their brief stay in Bethlehem to be taxed, after which they then returned to Nazareth. The Matthew Gospel says simply that Jesus was born in Bethlehem and had to be taken to Egypt. Only after returning from Egypt did his parents settle in Nazareth to allow Jesus, the reincarnated Zarathustra, to grow up in close proximity to the other, Buddhist current of Christianity. On a concrete level, the two worldviews were brought together. The Gospels show us the full depth of these events.

When the Gospels were written, people who understood the mysteries of existence knew that human abilities closely associated with strength and will — with the kingly element, to use the word in a specialized sense — were transmitted through physical heredity by the paternal element, while everything related to the inner element, to wisdom and inner mobility of spirit, was transmitted by the maternal element. Goethe, who saw so deeply into the mysteries of existence, draws our attention to this connection, saying:

> From Father I have stature
> For the seriousness of life
> From Mother a happy nature
> And a love for storytelling[2]

— a truth that you can often see confirmed. A person's stature — that is, everything expressed directly in the material figure of a human being — and "life's earnest conduct," which has to do with the character of the I, are inherited from the paternal element. Because his mission had always been to guide divine forces radiating through space into the human world, the Solomonic Jesus had to inherit his strength primarily from the paternal element. The writer of the Matthew Gospel expresses this fact in the greatest possible way: when the incarnation of this exceptional individuality is proclaimed as a significant event by the spiritual world, the announcement is received not by Mary but by the child's father, Joseph (Matt. 1:20-21). We cannot dismiss this fact as coincidence, for the story conceals profound truths. In contrast, the Nathanic Jesus received inner attributes, which are transmitted through the maternal line of descent, so his birth had to be announced to his mother, as in the Annunciation described in the Luke Gospel (Luke 1:26-38). These facts are expressed in the Scriptures in very profound ways.

Let's look at other, similarly significant facts described in the Gospels. The first is the appearance of John the Baptist as the forerunner of Jesus of Nazareth. We will discuss the individuality of the Baptist in greater detail later. For the moment, let's simply consider the image he presents as he proclaims what is to come in the person of Jesus. With infinitely great strength, John summarizes everything contained in the law, the old revelation. The Baptist's message is observance of the law, respect for the old, mature aspect of culture that people have forgotten. To proclaim this message, the Baptist needed above all else the strength of a soul born mature or over-mature. Here again, the Luke Gospel reveals a profound wisdom (Luke 1:18).

To ensure that from the very beginning, his astral body would be clean and free of all the forces that drag human beings down, John the Baptist was born to an elderly couple in whom desire and passion no longer played a role. The great mother lodge of humanity, where the great initiate Manu directs and guides processes in the spirit, looks after individuals such as John the Baptist, sending spiritual currents where they are needed. The incarnation of an I such as that of the Baptist was directly guided by the great mother lodge of humanity, the center of spiritual life on earth. The John-I and the soul of the Luke Jesus both originated in this mystery center, although the qualities Jesus received were not yet pervaded by the egotistic I — that is, the being guided toward incarnation as the reborn Adam was a young soul.

The reality of this situation, strange as it may seem, was that the great mother lodge sent out a soul unaccompanied by an actual developed I, for the same I that was reserved for the Jesus of the Luke Gospel was bestowed on the body of John the Baptist, and these two elements — the soul being that lived in the Luke Jesus and the I that lived in the Baptist — were intimately related from the very beginning. When a human embryo develops in the mother's body, the I unites with the other members of the human constitution as early as the third week. Its effects are felt only gradually, however, in the last months before birth, when it is internalized as a force that provokes movement. Typically, an I that originated in earlier incarnations stimulates the fetus to move. John's I, however, was intimately related to the soul-being of the Nathanic Jesus. That is why, as the Luke Gospel tells us, the mother of Jesus had to visit Elizabeth, John's mother, when the latter was in her sixth month of pregnancy. In this instance, the fruit of

Mary's womb provided the stimulus to movement normally supplied by the baby's own I. Elizabeth's child began to move as the woman carrying the infant Jesus approached, because the Jesus child was in fact the I that stimulated the other child to move (Luke 1:39-44). This indicates the deep connection between the being who merges the two spiritual currents and the one who proclaims his coming.

As we see, the beginning of our era was marked by a great and exceptional event. Lazy people who prefer not to formulate many concepts would like the truth to be simple. To perceive the greatest truths, however, we need to exert our intellectual and spiritual powers to the utmost. Since even describing a machine requires considerable effort on our part, we have no right to expect the greatest truths to be the simplest. The truth is great and therefore complex, and we must exert our spiritual forces if we truly want to learn the truth about the event in Palestine. I am not making these issues unnecessarily complicated, I am simply describing them as they are. We are dealing with the greatest facts in the earth's evolution, and they cannot be simplified.

So the two Jesus children grew up in Nazareth. One, the son of the Nathanic Joseph and Mary, was born to a young mother — the Hebrews would have used the word *alma* to describe her — because to function as a young soul, a being must be born to a very young mother. This boy lived with his parents after they returned to Nazareth from Bethlehem. They had no other children; his mother was allowed to devote herself entirely to the boy Jesus. Then there was the Jesus born to the Solomonic Joseph and Mary. After they returned from Egypt and settled in Nazareth, they had a number of other children whom the Mark Gospel lists: Simon, Judas, Joseph,

Jacob, and two sisters (Mark 6:3). As the two Jesus children grew up, the child who carried the Zarathustra individuality matured extremely quickly and developed the forces needed when such a mighty individuality is active in a body. The individuality active in the body of the other Jesus was very different in character. Its most important aspect, of course, was the Buddha's Nirmanakaya, which had overshadowed the child since birth. That is why we are told that the boy, at the time when his parents returned from Jerusalem, was "filled with wisdom" — that is, wisdom pervaded his ether body — and that "the favor of God was upon him" (Luke 2:40). As he grew up, however, he was exceptionally slow to develop ordinary human qualities related to understanding the material world. Superficial people, considering only the forces needed to grasp the outer world, would have called this boy mildly retarded. In contrast, however, he cultivated what flowed down from the Buddha's Nirmanakaya, developing incomparable depths of inwardness and feeling that had an exceptionally strong effect on his entire surroundings. Thus we see that the Nathanic Jesus matured into a being of deep feeling, while the Solomonic Jesus became an individuality of great maturity and profound understanding.

Words of great significance had been spoken to the mother of the Nathanic Jesus, the child of deep feeling. When Simeon met the newborn, illumined by an element Asita had not lived to see in the Buddha in India, he foretold the great and mighty events that would come to pass, but he also spoke great and significant words to the child's mother, "and a sword shall pierce through your own soul also" (Luke 2:35). Today we will also learn what these words meant.

The two children grew up in the same vicinity, and their

parents were friends. The Gospel reports that when the Nathanic Jesus approached his twelfth year, his parents went to Jerusalem to observe the Passover festival, taking the boy with them, as was the custom when children came of age. The Luke Gospel gives an extremely mysterious account of what then happened to the twelve-year-old Jesus in the temple. After leaving the festival and starting for home, his parents suddenly missed the boy; finding him nowhere among their traveling companions, they returned to Jerusalem and found him in the Temple surrounded by the great teachers, astonishing them all with his wisdom (Luke 2:41-50).

What had happened? Let's ask the immortal Akashic record. Facts of cosmic importance are not simple, but what happened in the Temple has been known to occur elsewhere in a somewhat different fashion. At a certain stage of development, an individuality may require circumstances different from those provided at birth. In the occasional case, a person grows and develops up to a certain age and then suddenly falls down unconscious and appears to be dead. A transformation then occurs; the person's own I departs and another I occupies the body. Other cases of I-transfer have been reported; the phenomenon is known to every occultist. What happened to the twelve-year-old Jesus was this: The Zarathustra I-being, having achieved the highest development possible at that time in the body of the Jesus descended from the kingly or Solomonic branch of the house of David, left that body and entered the Nathanic Jesus, who then appeared transformed. His parents did not recognize him and did not understand the words the Zarathustra-I spoke from within the Nathanic Jesus. At the very moment when the Zarathustra-I united with the Nathanic Jesus, the Buddha's Nirmanakaya also united with the boy's discarded maternal astral covering. The Zarathustra-I now lived in the Nathanic Jesus, transforming him to such an extent that his parents could not understand the boy they took home with them.

A short time later, the mother of the Nathanic Jesus died. We will see later that her death points to a particularly deep relationship. The other child, abandoned by the Zarathustra-I, also could not survive for long under ordinary circumstances. The Solomonic Joseph had died earlier, so the Nathanic Joseph took the mother of the Solomonic Jesus into his house, along with her sons Jacob, Joseph, Judas, and Simon, and her two daughters. The two families became one, and Zarathustra was once again surrounded by his birth family, with the exception of his father. His mother and siblings, as we can call them, since they were I-relatives although not blood relatives, lived in the Nathanic Joseph's house with the Jesus who was, at least in body, a native of Nazareth.

These complicated family circumstances represent the concrete confluence of Buddhism and Zoroastrianism. A single body received the mature I-soul of Zarathustra and united it with the product of the merger of the Buddha's Nirmanakaya with the discarded maternal astral covering of the Nathanic Jesus. In other words, the maturing individuality of Jesus of Nazareth incorporated the Zarathustra I-being, which was illumined and imbued with spirit by the rejuvenated Nirmanakaya of the Buddha. Thus the confluence of Buddhism and Zoroastrianism became a living reality in the soul of Jesus of Nazareth. Because the Nathanic Joseph also died relatively early, the Zarathustra child was truly orphaned. In spirit, he was the reincarnation of Zarathustra, not the person he was according to his physical lineage. According to his bodily line of descent, he was the son of the Nathanic Joseph, and to physical perception, that is who he was. Luke describes this situation exactly, and we must take his words literally:

> Now when all the people were baptized, and when Jesus also had been baptized and was praying, the heaven was opened, and the Holy Spirit descended upon him in bodily form, as a dove, and a voice came from heaven, "Thou art my beloved son; today I have begotten thee." Jesus, when he began his ministry, was about thirty years of age (Luke 3:21-23).

In a subsequent verse, instead of simply stating that Jesus was the son of Joseph, the Gospel says, "being the son (as was supposed) of Joseph," because essentially his I, which had originally incarnated in the Solomonic Jesus, had nothing to do with the Nathanic Joseph.

The being of Jesus of Nazareth had already united the great and mighty inner forces of Buddhism and all the blessings of Zoroastrianism. His inwardness would later be called upon to fulfill a great and mighty destiny very different from that of others baptized by John in the Jordan. As we will see later, this inwardness received the Christ at the baptism in the Jordan. At the same time, the immortal aspect of the birth mother of the Nathanic Jesus descended upon the mother whom the Nathanic Joseph had taken into his house and made her virginal again. Thus the soul of the mother he had lost was restored to Jesus during the baptism. His remaining mother sheltered the soul of his birth mother, the Mary whom the Bible calls "blessed among women" (Luke 1:28).

BASEL, SEPTEMBER 19, 1909

NOTES

1. Literally, "From among the lesser ancillary organs of the animals, light has called forth one organ to become its like, and thus the eye is formed by the light and for the light so that the inner light may emerge to meet the outer light." *Goethes Naturwissenschaftliche Schriften* ("Goethe's Scientific Works"), edited and with commentary by Rudolf Steiner, five volumes in the Kürschner series *Deutsche National-Literatur* ("German National Literature"), 1884-1897, reprinted as GA 1 a-e, Dornach 1975. This quotation appears in the chapter entitled *Entwurf einer Farbenlehre. Didaktischer Teil. Einleitung* ("Introduction to a Proposed Theory of Color; Didactic Section"), p. 88. The translation above is from J. W. von Goethe, *Scientific Studies*, vol. 12, editor and translator Douglas Miller. New York: Suhrkamp, 1988, p. 164.

2. The German quotation is from *Zahme Xenien* ("Gentle Satires") 6, no. 32 in the Kürschner edition (Deutsche National-Literatur) of Goethe's works (vol. 3, 1). It appears in English in Rudolf Steiner, *The Education of the Child*, Hudson N.Y.: Anthroposophic Press, 1996.

SIX

Elijah, John the Baptist, and Zarathustra

I HOPE YOU WILL NOT be annoyed by the amount of background material that we will have to cover today. It will be relatively easy to understand the details of the Luke Gospel if we first learn who we are dealing with, that is, if we do the preliminary work of bringing the Gospel's beings and individualities to life in our souls. We will never grasp what the Luke Gospel tells us in such simple and straightforward terms without first becoming aware of the full complexity of the Gospel's great central figure, along with a few other issues. Before we do so, however, we must recall a subject that we discussed in the last few days, namely, the great significance of the unique being who rose from bodhisattvahood to buddhahood five or six centuries before the beginning of the

Christian era. Let's look again at what this being meant to humankind.

The content of the Buddha's teachings had to be transferred to humankind and transformed into the personal possession of individuals. In all epochs of human history prior to the life of the Buddha, no human beings on earth could discover for themselves the Buddha's message of compassion and love as stated in the eightfold path. Humankind had not yet evolved to the point where each individual soul could discover these truths through meditation on its own thoughts and feelings. Phenomena must evolve, and each evolutionary accomplishment enters existence at a specific time and as a consequence of a specific cause. In that case, how could people in earlier times follow the precepts of the eightfold path, for example? They could do so only by receiving these principles from above, through initiates and seers in the esoteric schools. The bodhisattva taught in these mystery centers because they enabled human souls to ascend to higher worlds to receive teachings that could not yet be presented exoterically to independent human reasoning. These teachings had to be instilled in the rest of humankind by a privileged few who had direct contact with esoteric teachers. Ordinary individuals had to conduct their lives according to spiritual, moral principles, yet without being able to discover these principles for themselves. Those who lived outside the mystery centers received such principles unconsciously from others who transmitted them, also unconsciously, from the esoteric schools.

At that time, the content of the eightfold path had to be revealed from above because not even the most spirit-filled human body on earth could have discovered it independently. Consequently, prior to the life of the Buddha, a being such as the bodhisattva could not utilize a human body fully because no suitable human body existed. No human body could embody all the faculties that such a being needed in order to influence humankind. What had to happen to change this state of affairs? How did the bodhisattva manage to incarnate? Let's consider these questions.

Initially, the being of the bodhisattva did not incarnate fully into a human body. Clairvoyant perception would have revealed that a body ensouled by a bodhisattva included only part of his spiritual being, while his ether body extended far beyond the physical body to maintain contact with the spiritual element that the bodhisattva never completely left. He lived simultaneously in a spirit body and in a physical body. The transition from bodhisattva to buddha meant that this being descended fully into a physical human body for the first time. In doing so, he presented an ideal human figure for others to emulate so that they too could independently discover the teachings of the eightfold path, just as he himself had seen his own inner resources emerge as he sat under the *bodhi* tree. If we examine the earlier incarnations of the being who eventually became the Buddha, we discover that part of his being had to remain in the spiritual world while another part incarnated in a physical body. The first human constitution able to fully incorporate this bodhisattva-being became available only in the fifth or sixth century before Christ. Only then was the Buddha able to provide an example for humankind to follow in discovering the eightfold path from within, in the individual soul's own morality.

The phenomenon of human beings who lived partially in the spiritual world had always been acknowledged by all religions and worldviews. These worldviews recognized that hu-

man existence was too restrictive to encompass the full individualities of some beings who needed to work on earth. In
the Near East, the state of connection between a higher individuality and a physical body was called "being filled with the
Holy Spirit." This is a very specific technical term. In the customary usage of Near Eastern languages, a being incarnated
in the manner of a bodhisattva was said to be "filled with the
Holy Spirit" — that is, the forces comprising such a being were
not fully embodied by the being, who was influenced by an
external spiritual element. Therefore, we might say that in his
previous incarnations, the Buddha had been filled with the
Holy Spirit.

Having understood this state, we can also make sense of a
situation that we mentioned yesterday when considering the
beginning of the Luke Gospel. We heard that the human ether
body's previously untouched portion, which had been rescued
from the event we call the Fall — in other words, etheric substance taken from Adam before the Fall — was preserved and
inserted into the ether body of the child Jesus who was the
physical offspring of the Nathanic branch of the house of
David. This necessary happening produced a young being who
was untouched by all the events of earthly evolution and receptive to a great destiny. Could the Buddha's Nirmanakaya
have overshadowed an ordinary human being who had incarnated repeatedly since Lemurian times? Never! And it would
have been even less possible for such an individual to receive
what was to come later. A suitably ennobled human body could
be produced only by incorporating the etheric substance taken
from Adam, which had remained untouched by all earthly
events, into the ether body of this particular Jesus child.[1] This
etheric substance was bound up with all the forces that influ-

enced the earth's evolution before the Fall, and these forces generated mighty powers in the Nathanic infant Jesus and allowed his mother to have a remarkable effect on John the Baptist's mother and her unborn child, as we mentioned.

At this point we must also clarify the nature of the being we encounter in John the Baptist. We can understand John fully only by recalling the difference between the unique revelation that Indians received through the Buddha and the revelation the ancient Hebrew people received through Moses and his successors, the Hebrew prophets. Through the Buddha, humankind acquired the lawfulness that each soul discovers for itself and uses to purify itself and rise to the highest possible level of earthly morality. As proclaimed by the Buddha, *dharma*, the law of the soul, is accessible to individual human souls at the highest level of development; the Buddha was the first to derive it from within. Human evolution, however, does not proceed in a straight line, and very different cultural currents must fructify each other. The impending Christ event in the Near East required the culture of that region to remain behind that of India. The Near East had to produce an ethnic group that evolved very differently, remaining behind the peoples of the Orient. This evolutionary delay would later make Near Eastern culture freshly receptive to gifts that had been bestowed on Indian culture earlier and in a different form. While cosmic wisdom guided Indians toward beholding the bodhisattva as the Buddha, the peoples of the Near East, especially the ancient Hebrews, had to remain behind at a lower, more childlike level.

This delay in their evolution was necessary and inevitable. If it had not occurred, we would have seen a phenomenon on a large scale — that is, in human evolution — that can be observed on a smaller scale in young adults with acquired abilities that shackle or impede their owners in certain respects. A unique attribute of faculties acquired at this stage of life is that they tend to restrict their possessors to their current level, making it difficult for thirty-year-olds to transcend the level of development they achieved at age twenty. In contrast, consider a twenty-year-old who has achieved relatively little through personal effort but acquires these same faculties from others at a later age. Such an individual, who remains child-like longer, achieves the twenty-year level more easily and is more likely to transcend it at age thirty. These statements are confirmed by true observations of human life. Abilities that we acquire through early personal efforts constitute a greater obstacle than those we acquire by outer means later, when they are less closely linked to our own souls.

Human progress depends on recurrences of a large-scale phenomenon in which one cultural current incorporates certain faculties while the development of a parallel current is delayed. The first current develops its faculties to a particular level, linking them inextricably to that culture's articulation of human nature. Time passes, and when something new appears, the first current's inner resources do not allow it to advance to a higher level. Instead, the impetus passes to the parallel current, which had remained undeveloped in certain respects, not even approaching the level of the first. This second current then incorporates all the accomplishments of the first as it moves on to achieve a still higher level through the youthful qualities it had preserved. As you see, one current fructifies the other. The spiritual powers guiding the cosmos must ensure the presence of parallel currents in human evolution.

How could the guiding powers ensure that the current exemplified by the great Buddha would be paralleled by a current that only later embraced Buddhism's gifts to humankind? Only by making it impossible for the other current, which we know as ancient Hebrew culture, to produce individuals capable of following the eightfold path or developing *dharma* through individual, internalized morality. Ancient Hebrew culture could not have a buddha. For this culture, morality — which the Buddha had achieved on behalf of his cultural current as a matter of individual inwardness — had to come from outside. Long before the Buddha's appearance in India, this wise course of events was preordained by the exoteric revelation of the Decalogue, or Ten Commandments, to this Near Eastern ethnic group. The Hebrews received the Ten Commandments, a summation of all outer laws, from outside rather than from within. The gift of morality was neither closely tied to the individual soul nor experienced as an inner, personal possession as it was in the other cultural current. Because of their childlike stage of evolution, the ancient Hebrews experienced the law as a gift from heaven. The recognition that individuals produce *dharma*, the law of the soul, from within themselves, was cultivated in the Indian people, whereas obedience to a law bestowed from outside was cultivated in the Hebrews. The Hebrew people formed a wonderful complement to what Zarathustra had accomplished on behalf of his own culture and all the cultures that emerged from it.

In previous lectures, we emphasized that Zarathustra directed his students' attention to the outer world. While the Buddha offered incisive teachings about the ennoblement of the inner human being, Zarathustra offered great and mighty cosmological teachings and insight into the world from whose womb we emerge. While the Buddha's gaze turned inward, members of Zarathustra's culture turned to the outer world to understand its spiritual foundations.

Let's reflect deeply on Zarathustra's gift from the incarnation when he proclaimed Ahura Mazda to his next appearance as Nazarathos. In the interim, his teachings about great spiritual laws and the beings of the cosmos became more vivid. In a certain respect, Zarathustra simply identified the great spirit of the sun during his Persian incarnation but fleshed out his indications with Chaldean teachings about the cosmos and the spiritual origins of humankind. These cosmological teachings are wonderful but difficult to understand today. On close examination, they reveal an important idiosyncrasy.

When Zarathustra taught the ancient Persians about the sense-perceptible world's external spiritual origins, he introduced them to the two opposing cosmic powers of Ormuzd and Ahriman, or Angramainyu. There is no soul-warming morality in these teachings. According to ancient Persian views, human beings are embedded in cosmic processes; the conflict between Ormuzd and Ahriman is staged in the human soul, where it causes raging human passions. Zarathustra's cosmic teachings do not yet acknowledge the individual soul's inwardness. When the Persians spoke of good and evil, they meant useful and harmful influences that oppose each other in the cosmos and also manifest in human beings. In certain respects, Zarathustra's teachings about the nonhuman world did not yet incorporate a moral worldview, although they described all the useful, light-filled beings and dark, harmful beings governing the sense-perceptible world. The Persians experienced their own involvement in the activity of these beings, but they did not experience personal morality with any of the intensity of later cultures. For example, they felt that all "evil" human beings they encountered were "possessed" by evil cosmic beings — that is, that humans received evil forces from evil spiritual beings and were not responsible for evil in themselves. The Persians experienced human beings as embedded in a world not yet imbued with moral qualities. Even when they directed people's spiritual gaze outward, Zarathustra's teachings were distinctively amoral.

Hebrew teachings formed a wonderful complement to Zarathustra's cosmology because they added a moral element to external revelation, giving meaning to the concept of human guilt. Previously, evil human beings had simply been considered to be possessed by evil forces. The unveiling of the Ten Commandments made it necessary for people to distinguish between observers of the law and nonobservers, and the concept of human guilt or indebtedness emerged. We can sense the entry of this concept into human evolution when we recall a clear and tragic portrayal of unclarity about the concept of guilt. A receptive mind notes this unclarity in the book of Job. A new concept of guilt begins to illuminate Job's uncertainty about how to deal with misfortune.

Of all ethnic groups, the Hebrews in particular were given morality as a revelation from outside, like revelations about the nonhuman kingdoms of nature. This new moral revelation was possible only because Zarathustra, concerned about the continuation of his work, transferred his astral body to Hermes and his ether body to Moses. This ether body allowed Moses to perceive events in the outer world as Zarathustra had. Rather than perceiving them as arbitrary, neutral forces, however, he also sensed the moral governance of the world, which can become law. This is why ancient Hebrew culture embraced the virtue of obedience, or submission to the law, whereas the Buddhist spiritual current embraced the ideal of the eightfold path as a direction for human life.

The ancient Hebrew people, however, also had to endure until the Christ-principle appeared at the time we are describing in these lectures. Their culture was meant to be spared the Buddha's revelation, so to speak, and to persist at a lower level of maturity. To this end, no Hebrew personality could be capable of supporting the full, complete being of an individuality exemplifying the law. A personality like the Buddha could not appear among the Hebrews. They had received the law through external enlightenment, through Zarathustra's ether body in Moses, which made Moses receptive to a law that he did not conceive in his own soul. The Hebrews could not conceive the law in their own hearts. Nevertheless, the work of Moses, like any other work, had to be carried on so that it would bear the right fruit at the right time. That is why the individualities known as prophets and seers appeared among the ancient Hebrews. The individual we call Elijah was one of the most important of these seers.

How must we imagine such a personality? He was one of those chosen to represent Mosaic law to the Hebrew people. No human being of Hebrew descent, however, could completely exemplify the law of Moses, which the Hebrews received only as a revelation from above. The unique nature of the bodhisattva was a necessity in Indian culture, and the Hebrews, too, needed the repeated appearance of individualities who were not totally subsumed by their human personalities, who incarnated only partially into personalities on the physical plane while reserving another aspect of their being for the spiritual world. Elijah was one such being whose I-being could not totally penetrate his physical body. As I said earlier, such personalities were said to be "filled with the Holy Spirit."

The normal forces that prompt human incarnation on earth were inadequate to induce an incarnation such as Elijah's. Normally, when earthly birth approaches, the reincarnating individuality simply unites at a specific moment with the physical being that develops in the mother's womb. In an ordinary case, this process is straightforward and does not require the intervention of any exceptional forces, but this is not the case with individualities like Elijah. Forces concerned with the part of the individuality that extends into the spiritual world must intervene in such incarnations. External forces influence the developing physical beings to such an extent that the individualities in question incarnate as inspired, ecstatic, or seemingly spirit-driven personalities whose knowledge greatly exceeds the capacity of their ordinary intelligence. Every Old Testament prophet was such a personality. The spirit-driven I could not always account for its actions. The spirit lived in the prophet's personality but was sustained from outside.

Personalities like this retreat into solitude from time to time. The portion of the I that is used by the personality then withdraws, inducing ecstatic and unconscious states, and the spirit speaks into the person from outside. Elijah was especially receptive to inspiration from above. His actions, his speech, and his gestures originated not only in the part of the I that inhabited his body but also in divine-spiritual beings who disclosed themselves through him.

The Gospels themselves tell us that the Elijah-being was to reincarnate in the child who was born to Zacharias and Elizabeth.[2] In previous incarnations, this individuality had not learned to activate his own I through the forces inherent in a normal incarnation process. Typically, the inner power of the I begins to stir as a person's physical human body develops in the mother's womb. In earlier incarnations, Elijah's individuality had not yet descended far enough to experience this connection. Unlike an ordinary I, which sets itself in motion, his I had always been stimulated from outside, and this stimulation had to be repeated in his incarnation as John the Baptist, even though John's I was further removed from the spiritual world and closer to the earth than the beings who had previously guided Elijah. The time had come for the Buddha-current to unite with the Zarathustra-current, and their rejuvenation was imminent. In that incarnation, the being who worked on John from outside had to be closely related to the earth and its concerns — as closely related as the Buddha, whose Nirmanakaya was now linked to the Nathanic Jesus and hovered above his head. The Buddha was connected to the earth in one sense but removed from it in another because he had risen into the heights and worked only through a Nirmanakaya, which inhabited a region "beyond" the earth. This was the being who had to work from outside to stimulate John the Baptist's I.

Just as spiritual forces had previously stimulated Elijah, transporting him into ecstatic states in which the divinity spoke through him, filling his I with a real force that he could then convey to the outer world, another spiritual being — the Buddha's Nirmanakaya, which hovered above the Nathanic Jesus — now stimulated the I of John the Baptist. The Buddha's Nirmanakaya affected Elizabeth as John's birth approached, stimulating movement in the fetus and awakening the baby's I in the sixth month of pregnancy. This being was closer to the earth and therefore actually shaped John's I instead of simply inducing inspiration, as had happened to Elijah. Influenced by the visit of the woman the Gospels call Mary, the I of John the Baptist began to stir. The I of the former Elijah, now John's I, was awakened and liberated by the Buddha's Nirmanakaya, which influenced John right down to the level of physical substance.

What consequences can we anticipate from this event? The mighty words Elijah spoke in the ninth century before Christ were actually God's words and his gestures God's gestures. Something similar was true of John the Baptist, since Elijah's experience was reenlivened in him. John's I was inspired by the content of the Buddha's Nirmanakaya. The power of this being, which revealed itself to the shepherds and hovered over the Nathanic Jesus, streamed into John the Baptist. Consequently, John's preaching is a revival of the Buddha's sermon.

In his uniquely moving sermon at Benares, the Buddha spoke of life's suffering and of the soul's search for release from suffering through the eightfold path. In such sermons, the Buddha proclaimed the eightfold path that he had recognized and often continued, saying: Until now, you have known only the teachings of the Brahmins, who trace their ancestry to Brahma himself and claim superiority to other human beings because of their noble origin. The Brahmins say that human worth is based on ancestry, but I tell you that human worth is based not on ancestry but on what individuals make of themselves. Individuals become worthy of the world's great wisdom through what they make of themselves.

The Buddha aroused the Brahmins' wrath by pointing to individual worth, saying: Truly, I tell you, it is not important to call yourself a Brahmin. It is important to purify yourself through your own personal forces. This is the spirit if not the letter of many of the Buddha's speeches. He usually went on to show that by understanding the world of suffering, we learn to experience compassion and become comforters and helpers, empathizing with the fate of others because we know that we ourselves feel the same pain and suffering.

At the time we are discussing, the Buddha lived in a Nirmanakaya, illumining the Nathanic Jesus and renewing his preaching through words he inspired in John the Baptist. The Buddha's words seem to flow from John's mouth when he says, for example: Who brought you to this point, you who refer to the 'wisdom of the snake'? You make much of being descended from the 'children of the snake,' as they are known in the service of the spiritual powers; you believe you offer fruits worthy of repentance simply by saying that you have Abraham for your father.[3] John elaborated on the Buddha's sermon, saying, Do not say that Abraham is your father, but become truly human regardless of your station in life. A worthy human being can be awakened in place of the stone beneath your feet. I tell you God can make children of Abraham out of these stones (Luke 3:7-8). And then he said, in the spirit of the Buddha's sermon, "He who has two coats, let him share with him who has none" (Luke 3:11). People came to him asking, "Teacher, what shall we do?" (Luke 3:12) just as the monks once asked the Buddha. All John's words seem to repeat or elaborate on the Buddha's words.

Through these beings who appeared on the physical plane at the beginning of the Christian era, we begin to understand the unity of all religions and spiritual revelations to humankind. We understand the Buddha not by clinging to tradition but by listening to his actual words. The Buddha gave his sermon at Benares five or six centuries before Christ. He did not fall silent after that lifetime, however. Although no longer incarnated, he continued to speak through others inspired by his Nirmanakaya. From the mouth of John the Baptist, we hear what the Buddha had to say six hundred years after the end of his final life in a physical body. Such is the unity of all religions. Because religions continue to evolve, we must look at each religion at the right point in human evolution and learn to understand its living aspects. Refusing to hear the Buddha in John the Baptist is like coming back to a blooming rosebush after having seen it in bud and refusing to believe that the flowers emerged from those buds. The living bud of the sermon at Benares bloomed when John preached at the Jordan.

The Luke Gospel speaks vividly of John, introducing us to the true being of another individuality of the early Christian era. We familiarize ourselves with the Gospels only when we rise to an understanding of each word's intended meaning. Luke's introduction states that he will recount the communications of "independent seers." These independent seers, however, did not simply see events on the physical plane. They saw the true circumstances that were gradually revealed through the ages. If we see only events on the physical plane, all we can say about the occurrences described in these lectures is that the son of King Suddhodana, who was later called the Buddha, lived five or six centuries before the time of John the Baptist. We overlook a link between these personalities that is visible only in the spiritual world. Luke, however, says that his story is based on the accounts of seers. Simply hearing the words of religious documents is not enough; we must learn to read their true meaning by make the individualities they describe come alive in our souls. To do so, we must learn what flowed into these individualities.

The body's faculties define the further development of any individuality incarnating on earth. Every incarnating being must reckon with this state of affairs. An exalted being descending today would be subject to the inherent lawfulness of a modern human body. The spiritual world really does not look like the physical world, and only seers, who see the finer threads of destiny, can identify an individuality's true being. The childhood of even a wise and exalted reincarnating being is spent preparing the body so that the essence of earlier incarnations can emerge at a certain point in time. A being whose task is to arouse specific sensations in human beings must incarnate in such a way that the body supports this mission. A being who wants to proclaim healing and release from pain and suffering must taste human suffering to the fullest extent in order to speak words meaningful to human beings.

The being cradled by the body of the Nathanic Jesus had a message to bring to all human beings, a message about transcending the old limitations of blood kinship. It was not meant to nullify blood relationships, to eliminate the bonds between father and son or brother and sister, but to supplement blood-bound love with a deeper universal human love that works from soul to soul, freed from all blood ties. This was the message and mission of the being who later appeared in the body of the Nathanic Jesus. To experience the connection between individuals in its pure form, this being had to feel firsthand the impact of having no blood relationships. He had to feel free of all blood ties and to know that such ties were impossible for him. The individuality of the Nathanic Jesus had to leave not only his home — like the Buddha, who left his palace for strange lands — but also all family ties and blood relationships. He had to experience all the profound pain of solitude and of bidding farewell to those closest to him. This individuality had to speak through the Nathanic Jesus from the perspective of great loneliness and familial abandonment.

Who was this being? We know that he was the individuality or spirit of Zarathustra, and that he was born to parents descended from Solomon and inhabited the body of the Solomonic Jesus for roughly the first twelve years of its life. His father died young, leaving the boy without one parent. As long as he lived in the body of the Solomonic Jesus, he belonged to a family that included other children, both brothers and sisters. At age twelve, he left his mother and siblings to enter the body of the Nathanic Jesus. His [Nathanic] mother died soon afterward, and later his [Nathanic] father. When he began his work in the world, he had lost all of his blood relatives. As the Zarathustra-being, he had not only been orphaned and obliged to leave his brothers and sisters but had also been denied the opportunity to marry and have children, because he had left even his own body behind in order to enter the body of the Nathanic Jesus. The Zarathustra-being paved the way for the still higher being who would later use the body of the Nathanic Jesus to prepare for his great mission of proclaiming universal human love. When the supposed mother and brothers of this being arrived to see him, he was told, "Your mother and brothers are standing outside, desiring to see you." For all the world to hear, from the depths of his soul, he denied their relationship unmistakably yet reverently, for he had relinquished even the body that was related to this family. Pointing to those who had freely chosen his company, he said,

"My mother and my brothers are those who hear the word of God and do it" (Luke 8:20-21). To this extent, the Scriptures must be taken literally.

The proclaimer of universal human love had to incarnate in a body that abandoned all blood ties. Our hearts respond to the human nearness of this figure who descended from lofty spiritual heights and to his expression of human experience and suffering. The better we understand this being on a spiritual level, the more our hearts and souls will acclaim him.

BASEL, SEPTEMBER 20, 1909

NOTES

1. In the German editions of 1949, 1955, and 1968, this sentence reads "astral body" instead of "ether body." Since the meaning of the sentence requires "ether body," the present edition reverts to the wording of the first three German editions.

2. Matt. 17:10-13: "And the disciples asked him, 'Then why do the scribes say that first Elijah must come?' He replied, 'Elijah does come, and he is to restore all things, but I tell you that Elijah has already come, and they did not know him, but did to him whatever they pleased. So also the Son of man will suffer at their hands.' Then the disciples understood that he was speaking to them of John the Baptist." See also the annunciation to Zechariah, Luke 1:17: "And he will go before him in the spirit and power of Elijah."

3. Cf. Matt. 3:7–8 and Luke 3:7–8.

SEVEN

Christ, the Great Mystery of Earth Evolution

IN THE PAST FEW DAYS, we pictured the Luke Gospel's most important beings and developed a comprehensive view of its spiritual foundations. One thing remains to be done, however. We must still trace the further evolution of Christ Jesus, the preeminent being in earth's history. We must first recall what we have already heard. Christ Jesus, as described in the Luke Gospel, was born in bodily form as the Nathanic Jesus of the house of David. This child grew and developed until about age twelve, when the being who had led Persian culture entered his body. Zarathustra's I lived in the Nathanic Jesus' body from its twelfth year onward.

Our previous anthroposophic studies have prepared us to follow the evolution of this being more exactly. We know that the first important period in normal human development encompasses the first seven years of life, the second, years seven to fourteen — the prepubescent years — and the next, years fourteen to twenty-one. A subsequent period lasts until year twenty-eight, and the next until thirty-five. These time periods, however, do not begin and end with pedantic precision. For example, the important transition around the seventh year of human development actually occurs by degrees during the second dentition, and the other transitions are similarly gradual. My booklet *The Education of the Child in the Light of Spiritual Science* describes the transition in the seventh year in greater detail.[1] This transition is an etheric birth of sorts. What happens then is comparable, on a higher level, to leaving the mother's womb at physical birth. Similarly, in the fourteenth year, at puberty, an astral birth occurs and the individual's astral body is set free. If we trace human development with precision, through the eyes of the spirit, it looks still more complicated. Important later transitions escape our ordinary observation. Today we tend to believe that individuals change relatively little after a certain age, but this belief is based on crude methods of observation. In reality, certain subtler changes in human development are evident to the appropriate modes of perception.

The body that is fully born when the protection of the mother's physical body is abandoned actually includes only the child's physical body. In the first seven years of life, only the physical body is fully emerged. (In various lectures on education, I emphasized the importance of this fact, especially for teachers.) Later, when the protection of the mother's etheric body is abandoned, the individual ether body is set free, and something similar happens to the astral body in the fourteenth year.

Strictly speaking, however, a complete understanding of the human constitution is based on the further subdivisions of the human soul that are listed in my book *Theosophy*.[2] The soul body, which forms a unity with the ether body or life body, is the first such subdivision. In precise terms, only the soul body is completely free before the twenty-first year. In the twenty-first year, the member that we call the sentient soul is gradually freed, while the mind soul or rational soul is freed at twenty-eight and the consciousness soul only later. This is how human development progresses at present. If our observation of human life is guided by spiritual scientific insight, we are well aware of these developmental stages. All of humankind's great leaders have also always known why the thirty-fifth year is so important. As we learn at the very beginning of the *Divine Comedy*, the cosmic visions Dante recorded in his great epic occurred during his thirty-fifth year.[3] Individuals at that developmental stage are fully able to use the faculties that relate to the soul body, sentient soul, and mind soul.

Teachers of human development have always been aware of these subdivisions of the human soul. The times are shifted somewhat in eastern cultures, accurately reflecting the somewhat different course of human development in the Orient, but the subdivisions are consistent throughout western civilization. The Greeks, for example, simply used somewhat different words for the phenomena we know today. In describing the human soul, they too began with the ether body, which they called *threptikon*. They applied the very descriptive term *aesthetikon* to what we call the soul body. The sentient soul was their *orektikon* and the mind soul *kinetikon*, and they called the consciousness soul, that most precious possession of modern human beings, *dianoetikon*. This is how human development appears to close observation.

As a result of circumstances that I will at least partially explain today, the Nathanic Jesus developed somewhat more quickly. Puberty typically occurred earlier in that part of the world, and individually specific reasons also contributed to an earlier transition. Consequently, the change that normally occurs in a child's fourteenth year happened in Jesus' twelfth year. Similarly, Jesus was nineteen when he underwent the transition that normally occurs in the twenty-first year, and he was twenty-six and thirty-three at the twenty-eight and thirty-five-year transitions, respectively. Here is a chart of the development of the central being of earthly evolution:

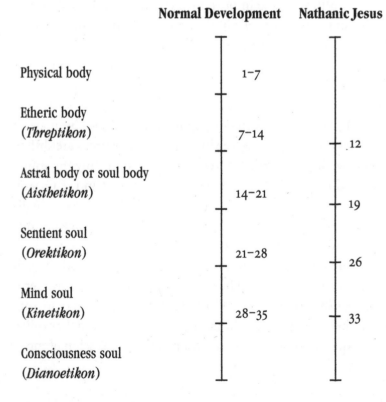

	Normal Development	**Nathanic Jesus**
Physical body	1–7	
Etheric body (*Threptikon*)	7–14	12
Astral body or soul body (*Aisthetikon*)	14–21	19
Sentient soul (*Orektikon*)	21–28	26
Mind soul (*Kinetikon*)	28–35	33
Consciousness soul (*Dianoetikon*)		

Please note that we are considering the body of the Nathanic Jesus, which Zarathustra's I inhabited from the twelfth year onward. What does that actually mean? It means simply that this mature — which, as we know, had experienced Zarathustra's destinies in different incarnations — cultivated the sentient body, sentient soul, and mind soul of the Nathanic Jesus as only a very mature I could do. We must grasp the wondrous fact that the Zarathustra-I incarnated into the body of the Nathanic Jesus in the twelfth year, developing Jesus' soul faculties with infinite subtlety. The soul body thus developed in Jesus looked out into the cosmos and beheld the spiritual being of the Ahura Mazda of old. His sentient soul harbored the knowledge and wisdom that human beings had gradually developed on the basis of Zarathustra's teachings about Ahura Mazda, and his mind soul learned to clothe everything that humankind had previously received only from external spiritual currents in easily understandable words and concepts. The Nathanic Jesus continued to develop under the influence of Zarathustra's I until a new change occurred as his thirtieth year approached. Once again, as at puberty, a new I filled the inner being of the Nathanic Jesus, but this time on a more universally significant level. Around the thirtieth year of Jesus' life, Zarathustra's I had finished incorporating all the gains of earlier incarnations into his soul and had developed his faculties to the highest possible level. This I, knowing that it had completed its mission with regard to that soul, subsequently left the body of the Nathanic Jesus.

As you recall, Zarathustra's I had inhabited the body of the other, Solomonic Jesus until approximately the twelfth year of life. When Zarathustra's I left him, the boy could not continue to develop but remained at his previous level, although admittedly he had achieved a rare and lofty degree of maturity while harboring such an exalted I. Anyone who observed the Solomonic Jesus boy even superficially would have seen an extremely precocious child. But as soon as he was abandoned by Zarathustra's I, the boy ceased to progress. A short time later, the mother of the Nathanic Jesus died. As her spiritual members were transported into the spiritual world, she took with her all the creative and eternally valuable forces of the Solomonic boy Jesus, who then died at approximately the same time.

A very precious etheric covering separated from the physical body of the Solomonic Jesus at death. Since the ether body accomplishes most of its development after a child's seventh year of life, in the period between the seventh year and puberty, the forces of Zarathustra's I had contributed to the development of this ether body. We know that when the ether body leaves the physical body at death at the end of a normal human life, everything not of eternal value is stripped away, leaving an extract of the ether body to persist from one incarnation to the next. The greatest possible portion of the Solomonic Jesus' ether body had acquired eternal value, and so the Nathanic mother took his entire life body with her into the spiritual world.

The ether body, however, sculpts and builds the human physical body. We can imagine the profound relationship between the Solomonic Jesus' ether body, now transported into the spiritual world, and Zarathustra's I, which had been united with it for twelve years of earthly life. When Zarathustra's I left the body of the Nathanic Jesus, the force of attraction between that I and the former ether body of the Solomonic Jesus reasserted itself, and these two members came together to build a new physical body. Zarathustra's I was so mature that it no longer had to pass through the devachan. In a relatively short time, with the help of the ether body we have just described, this I built a new physical body, resulting in the first birth of a being who subsequently reappeared repeatedly with relatively short intervals between physical death and rebirth. This being always reincarnated on earth very shortly after the death of the previous physical body.

Since that time, this being has reappeared consistently throughout human history, becoming, as you can well imagine, the great helper of all those seeking to understand the mighty event of Palestine. After rediscovering his former ether body, Zarathustra — that is, the Zarathustra — began a new career, wandering through the millennia of human history as the being called Master Jesus, who reincarnated repeatedly to guide and direct the spiritual current we call Christianity. This being inspires all attempts to understand the living, evolving Christianity. In esoteric schools, he inspired the ongoing cultivation of Christian teachings. Behind the great spiritual figures of Christianity stood this figure, constantly teaching the true significance of the great event of Palestine.

When Zarathustra's I, which had enlivened the body of the Nathanic Jesus from its twelfth to its thirtieth year, left that body, a different being incarnated. All the Gospels tell us that the highest I replaced Zarathustra's when Jesus was baptized in the Jordan by John. In my lectures on the John Gospel, I pointed out that baptism at that time, and as John performed it, was something completely different from the mere symbol it later became.[4] Candidates for baptism were totally submerged in the water. As you know from various preparatory anthroposophical lectures, this situation can provoke an extraordinary event. Even under normal circumstances, a person experiencing the shock of near-drowning may see a great tableau of his or her life to date. This tableau, which normally appears only at death, surfaces briefly when the ether body rises out of the physical body and is freed from its forces. Most of those baptized by John underwent such an experience, and the Nathanic Jesus was no exception. When his ether body left his physical body, the exalted being we call the Christ descended into the Nathanic Jesus and took possession of his body.

After baptism in the Jordan by John, therefore, the Nathanic Jesus was filled with the Christ being. This is the meaning of the words found in older manuscripts of the Gospels: "This is my dearly beloved son; today I have begotten him." The son of heaven, the Christ, had been conceived. The inseminator was the unitary divinity that weaves throughout the cosmos; the suitably prepared body and other constitutional members of the Nathanic Jesus received the divine seed from the heights. "This is my dearly beloved son; today I have begotten him" — this is what older manuscripts say and what newer versions of the Gospels should also say (Luke 3:22).

Who is the Christ being who united with the ether body of the Nathanic Jesus? We cannot understand him by looking only at earthly evolution, because he is the leader of the spiritual beings who separated from Earth along with the Sun in order to influence the earth from a higher, external vantage point. Thus in pre-Christian times, beginning with the Sun's separation from Earth, those who looked up at the Sun with sufficiently mature perception experienced what Zarathustra taught — that the sunlight and warmth that reach us are only the physical garments of exalted spiritual beings behind the sunlight, garments that conceal the spiritual forces irradiating the earth. All these beings send their beneficial influences down to Earth from the Sun, and their leader is the being we call the Christ. In pre-Christian times, this being could be found only on the Sun, not on Earth. Zarathustra was right when he pointed to the Sun as the dwelling place of the being called Ahura Mazda. Zarathustra said we cannot discover this being as we wander Earth, but only when we look up at the Sun. The spiritual being living in the Sun is Ahura Mazda, and the light that streams down to us is his body, just as the physical human body is the body of the human spirit. Through great cosmic events, this exalted being gradually approached the sphere of Earth. Clairvoyants could perceive his approach. The first clear recognition of the Christ occurred on Mount Sinai, when he was revealed to his great predecessor Moses in fire and lightning.

What do these revelations signify? They were like a reflection of the approaching Christ being, the spiritual counterpart of the reflected sun rays we see at each full moon. The light shining toward us is sunlight, but we call it moonlight because it is reflected by the Moon. Who did Moses see in the burning bush and in the fire on Mount Sinai? He saw the Christ! He saw the Christ's reflection, just as we see reflected sunlight when we look at the Moon. We call this reflected sunlight moonlight, and the people of that time called the Christ's reflection Yahweh or Jehovah. Just as sunlight announces its presence through moon rays at full moon, the Christ announced his presence indirectly because human beings could not yet perceive his actual being. Yahweh or Jehovah is the indirect, reflected light of the Christ before his appearance on Earth.

The Christ was destined to become ever more accessible to human perception and understanding. He was to live on earth, human among humans, revealing himself directly to all as he had previously revealed himself in the cosmos to initiates. Initiates with access to cosmic wisdom had always been aware of the Christ's existence, although they gave his different manifestations different names. To Zarathustra, he revealed himself in garments of sunlight, so Zarathustra called him Ahura Mazda. The holy *rishis*, the great teachers of humanity in ancient India during the first epoch after the Atlantean catastrophe, were also aware of this being, but they knew that he would remain inaccessible to earthly wisdom until a later epoch. The seven *rishis* said that he dwelled beyond their region and called him Vishva Karman. Vishva Karman and Ahura Mazda are different names for the same being, who was slowly approaching Earth from the spiritual heights of the cosmos.

Lengthy preparations were required to produce a body capable of receiving this being. First Zarathustra's I had to mature from incarnation to incarnation, eventually incarnating in the pure body of Jesus of Nazareth to refine the faculties of a soul body, sentient soul, and mind soul to receive such an exalted being. The preliminary steps took a long time. To learn to transform the faculties of the Nathanic Jesus, Zarathustra's I first had to undergo all the life experiences of several different incarnations. Furthermore, Zarathustra's I could not have performed this transformation at any earlier time, because the Nathanic child Jesus had to be shaped not only by Zarathustra but also by the exalted being we described as the Buddha's Nirmanakaya. But the Buddha's Nirmanakaya first had to exist! The bodhisattva had to achieve buddhahood before he could develop the spirit body, or Nirmanakaya, that would shape the Nathanic child Jesus between birth and puberty. Without first becoming a buddha, the bodhisattva would have lacked the strength to make that body sufficiently mature to support such a great occurrence. This capability developed only in the incarnation when the bodhisattva became the Buddha.

When we finally learn to understand the great wisdom preserved in ancient legends, we will find that they reflect the entire contents of the Akashic record in wondrous form. We are quite rightly told that as early as the ancient Indian epoch, human beings learned about the cosmic Christ being who dwelled outside the sphere of the seven holy *rishis*. The *rishis* knew that this being lived in the heights and was only gradually approaching Earth. Zarathustra also knew that he had to turn to the Sun to find this being, and the ancient Hebrews were the first to develop faculties that allowed them to perceive his reflection.

Legend tells us that as the bodhisattva was preparing to become a buddha, he was approached by Vishva Karman, who would later be called the Christ. As the bodhisattva's twenty-ninth year drew near, he made his first trip away from the palace where such great care and attention had been lavished upon him. He soon met an old man, then a sick person, and then a corpse, so he became aware of life's misery. He saw age, sickness, and death personified in a monk who had just departed this life. At this point — so the legend tells us in its great wisdom — he would have returned to the palace if Vishva Karman, the artist of the gods, had not appeared to him. Vishva Karman, who would later be called the Christ, sent his own forces down to Earth to adorn the young bodhisattva. The Christ was still an external presence to the bodhisattva. Like

Jesus of Nazareth at the baptism in the Jordan, the bodhisattva was approaching his thirtieth year, but he was not mature enough to completely receive the Christ in his human body. In his life as the Buddha, he achieved this maturity. When he reappeared in his Nirmanakaya, or spiritual body, his task was to prepare the body of the Nathanic Jesus, which he himself did not inhabit, to receive Vishva Karman, or the Christ. All the forces of Earth evolution worked together to bring about the great event of Christ's incarnation.

At this point, we may wonder how the Christ, or Vishva Karman, relates to beings such as the bodhisattvas, one of whom was the future Buddha. This question leads us to the brink of one of the greatest mysteries in earthly evolution. As a general rule, people with modern feelings and sensations have great difficulty achieving even an inkling of the power behind this mystery. In the entire cosmos to which our Earth belongs, there are twelve bodhisattvas. The one who became the Buddha five or six centuries before Christ was entrusted with the mission of teaching humankind to embody compassion and love. Just as his mission was to bring the doctrine of compassion and love to earth, each of the other bodhisattvas has a specific mission to accomplish in a different earthly epoch. The Buddha was especially close to the earth's overall mission because the development of moral attitudes was the task of our age, which extends from the time five or six centuries before Christ when the bodhisattva appeared to the time when he will be succeeded by the next bodhisattva, who will one day live on earth as the Maitreya Buddha. Earth evolution progresses because the bodhisattvas descend to earth at intervals to embody the contents of their mission. If we could survey the entire history of the earth, we would discover twelve bodhisattvas. As members of a mighty spiritual community, they are sent down to earth to serve as special messengers to humankind, as the great teachers of humanity. We must acknowledge the role of the great lodge of the twelve bodhisattvas in governing the entire evolution of the earth.[5] On a higher plane, the bodhisattvas manifest the concept of "teacher" as we apply it on lower levels of existence. As teachers, they inspire specific faculties that human beings must acquire. What is the source of the content the bodhisattvas proclaim from epoch to epoch? If you could behold the circle of the twelve bodhisattvas in the great spirit lodge, you would discover a thirteenth being sitting in their midst. This being, who cannot be called a teacher in the same sense as the twelve, radiates the substance of wisdom itself. The twelve bodhisattvas in the great spirit lodge sit around a central point, immersed in contemplation of the great being who exudes the wisdom that they are to incorporate into earthly evolution. The thirteenth being exudes what the other twelve will teach. The twelve are the teachers and inspirers who proclaim the presence of the thirteenth from epoch to epoch; the thirteenth is the very substance of their teaching. He is the ancient *rishis'* Vishva Karman, Zarathustra's Ahura Mazda, and our Christ, the leader and guide of the great bodhisattva lodge. Thus the entire choir of bodhisattvas proclaims the doctrine of the Christ, or Vishva Karman. The bodhisattva who became the Buddha five or six centuries before Christ was adorned with the forces of Vishva Karman. The Nathanic Jesus who received the Christ was not merely "adorned" but "anointed" — that is, pervaded by and imbued with Vishva Karman, the Christ.

A symbol or image appears wherever people sense this

great mystery or recognize it through initiation. Before the emergence of Christianity, for example, the little known, highly secretive Drotten mysteries of northern Europe created an earthly symbol of the spiritual reality of the lodge of the twelve bodhisattvas. The Drotten mysteries of ancient Europe always included a community of twelve teachers whose task was to convey spiritual knowledge. These communities also had a thirteenth member, not a teacher, whose mere presence radiated the wisdom the others received. This was an earthly image of a heavenly spiritual reality. *The Mysteries*, a poem that reflects Goethe's Rosicrucian inspiration, is another example of a community of twelve surrounding a thirteenth, who need not be a great teacher.[6] In this poem, the monks hail the simple Brother Markus as the successor of their deceased thirteenth member. The task of the thirteenth is not to present teachings but to be the teachings, to be spiritual substance itself. This has always been the case wherever people comprehend or divine this exalted reality.

The baptism in the Jordan, therefore, represents the point in human evolution when spiritual substance itself, the heavenly thirteenth being, appeared on earth. All other beings, both bodhisattvas and buddhas, taught about this being, and mighty preparations were required so that he could descend into a human body. This is the mystery of the baptism in the Jordan. The Gospels describe Vishva Karman, or Ahura Mazda, now called the Christ, in the body of the Nathanic Jesus. This being was to spend three years on earth as a human among humans, inhabiting a time-tested earthly entity with the thirty years of experience we described earlier. The Nathanic Jesus was irradiated and pervaded by a being who had previously been clothed in the radiant, warming sun rays shining down from the cosmos, a being who had left Earth when the Sun separated from it.

There is another question we must ask, namely, why did this being unite with the earth's evolution at such a late stage? Why didn't he descend to earth earlier? Why couldn't he occupy a human ether body earlier, before the baptism in the Jordan? We will understand why once we understand more exactly the event the Old Testament describes as the Fall. The event depicted symbolically as the Fall into sin in Paradise occurred in Lemurian times, when the human astral body was invaded by certain beings — the Luciferic beings — who had remained behind on the evolutionary level of the Old Moon. Because Luciferic forces invaded the human astral body, we humans became more deeply entangled in earthly affairs than we would have been otherwise. If we had not fallen under the influence of Lucifer, we would have completed our evolution on earth in higher spheres, as it were, less deeply involved in earthly matter. This influence made us descend to earth prematurely. If nothing else had happened to counteract the Luciferic forces that were in the human astral body, these forces would have invaded the ether body as well. As my book *An Outline of Esoteric Science* describes from a different perspective, the cosmic powers took exceptional measures to prevent this invasion. Human beings could not be permitted to remain as they were once the astral body accepted the Luciferic forces. To protect the ether body from the effect of these forces, human beings were made incapable of using the entire ether body. A portion of the ether body was placed out of reach of free human will. Without this benevolent divine act, human beings would have retained power over the entire ether body and would not have been able to continue to evolve appropriately

on earth. Certain aspects of the human ether body were rescued and saved for a later time. Let's attempt to view these
with the eyes of the spirit.

The human being includes the same states of matter that
we find in the world outside us — the earthly or solid element, the watery or liquid element, and the airy or gaseous
element. These elements constitute the human physical body
and all other physical objects. The etheric domain begins with
the first ether state, which we call the fire ether, or simply fire.
Fire or warmth, which modern physics sees as mere movement
rather than as substance, is really the first ether state. The second is the light ether, or light, and the third, imperceptible to
us in its original form, is the finer etheric or spiritual element
that underlies physical sound. The sound we perceive in the
physical world is a mere reflection or shadow of this ether state,
the sound or number ether. The fourth ether state is the life
ether, which underlies all life as such.

In the constitution of the modern human, all aspects of
the soul leave imprints on the physical and etheric bodies. Each
soul force is assigned to a specific etheric substance, so to speak.
What we call human will is expressed in the etheric element
of fire. If you are even slightly receptive to the connections
between certain sensations, you will sense that we are right in
speaking about the will in this way. The will, which expresses
itself physically in the blood, or in the movement of the blood,
lives in the etheric fire element, while what we call feeling is
expressed in the light ether within the ether body. This is why
clairvoyants perceive human will impulses as flames flickering in the ether body and radiating into the astral body, while
they perceive feelings as shapes made of light. As you can easily imagine, the thoughts we experience in our souls and ex-

press in the sounds of our words are mere shadowy images of thinking, because physical sound is also only a shadow image of a higher sound element, the sound ether that includes the organ for words. Our words, in turn, are underlain by thoughts; that is, words are means of expressing thoughts. These means of expression fill etheric space by sending their vibrations through the sound ether. Sound, however, is only a shadow of actual thought vibrations, but the inner aspect that gives our thoughts meaning belongs to the life ether.

Meaning	—	Life ether
Thinking	—	Sound ether
Feeling	—	Light ether
Will	—	Fire ether
		Air
		Water
		Earth

Of these four states of ether, only the lower two — the fire ether and the light ether — remained accessible to free human will in Lemurian times, while the two upper types were taken away from us. This is the inner meaning of the passage in Genesis: Human beings, having learned to distinguish between good and evil (symbolized by "eating of the tree of knowledge") under the influence of the Luciferic forces, had to be prevented from eating from the tree of life. That is, the part of the ether body that has free and independent access to the thought ether and the meaning ether was taken away from us, and only feeling and will remained subject to free choice. As a result, we can each express personal will and personal feelings. Feeling and willing remain freely accessible to the personal element in each human being, so our feelings and will impulses are individually different. The individual impulse stops short, however, when we rise from the feeling level to the thinking level or even to the expression of thinking — that is, to words on the physical plane. Feelings and intentions are personal matters for each of us, but we immediately enter a universal element when we rise into the world of words and thoughts. We cannot each make our own thoughts. If thoughts were as individual as feelings, we would never understand each other. Thus thought and meaning were removed from the realm of human free will and temporarily preserved in the sphere of the gods, to be returned to human beings later. Wherever we go on the face of the earth, we find individual human beings with individual feelings and will impulses, but thinking is the same everywhere and each ethnic group shares a common language governed by a common folk spirit. This sphere is inaccessible to human will; for now, the gods work into it.

When Zarathustra and his pupils pointed toward the kingdom of the spirit, they were right in calling the warmth, or fire, and light that stream down from heaven the garments of Ahura Mazda. These garments, however, conceal an undescended element that remains in spiritual heights, casting only a shadow into physical human thoughts and words. The Sun's warmth and light conceal the living aspects of sound and meaning, which are disclosed only to those who see behind the light. These living aspects relate to the earthly word as the heavenly word relates to the aspects of life that have been rescued temporarily from humankind. This is why Zarathustra told his pupils to look up to Ahura Mazda, to see how he reveals himself in the physical garments of light and warmth, which conceal the divine Word of creation that is approaching the earth.

What is Vishva Karman? What is Ahura Mazda? What is the Christ, in his true form, but the divine Word of creation? Strange as it may seem, Zoroastrianism tells us that Zarathustra was initiated so that he could perceive, standing behind the light, not only Ahura Mazda but also Honover, the divine Word of creation that was to descend to earth. During the baptism in the Jordan, this Word descended into an individual human ether body for the first time. The spirit Word that had been preserved since Lemurian times streamed down from the heights into the ether body of the Nathanic Jesus. When the baptism was completed, the Word had become flesh.

From the very beginning, Zarathustra and other seers who knew his secrets proclaimed the presence of the Word that is concealed behind warmth and light. These "independent seers" became the "servants of the Word" whose proclamations are recorded in the Luke Gospel.

This example demonstrates again that the Gospels must be taken literally. The element that had been denied human beings for so long because of their involvement with Lucifer first became flesh, descending to earth and living on earth, in a single personality. This being is the great ideal to be emulated by all those who slowly learn to understand his nature. This is why our earthly wisdom must follow the example of the bodhisattvas, whose task is always to proclaim the thirteenth in their midst. We must apply all our spiritual science — our wisdom, our knowledge, and the results of spiritual research — to comprehending the being and nature of Vishva Karman, Ahura Mazda, or the Christ.

BASEL, SEPTEMBER 20, 1909

NOTES

1. See note 1, lecture 4.

2. Rudolf Steiner, *Theosophy.* Hudson, N.Y.: Anthroposophic Press, 1994.

3. Dante Alighieri, Italian poet, 1265–1321. The great epic his contemporaries called the *Divina Commedia* was written between 1307 and 1321, during his years of travel (*Wanderjahre*).

4. See Rudolf Steiner, *The Gospel of St. John and Its Relation to the Other Gospels.* Spring Valley, N.Y.: Anthroposophic Press, 1982.

5. On the twelve bodhisattvas, see also Rudolf Steiner's lecture "Bodhisattvas, Buddhas, and Christ" (Milan, September 21, 1911) in: *From Buddha to Christ.* Hudson, N.Y.: Anthroposophic Press/London: Rudolf Steiner Press, 1987.

6. *The Mysteries: A Fragment* appears in Kürschner's Deutsche National-Litteratur edition of Goethe's works, volume 3, 1, H. Düntzer, ed. Part of this poem appears in a lecture by Rudolf Steiner, "The Mysteries: A Christmas and Easter Poem by Goethe." London: Rudolf Steiner Publishing Co., 1946 (Cologne, Dec. 25, 1907).

EIGHT

Illness and Healing in Luke and in the Evolution of Consciousness

We HAVE BEEN ATTEMPTING to picture the spiritual foundations of the first few chapters of the Luke Gospel. Understanding the Jesus of Nazareth who received the cosmic Christ principle in his thirtieth year requires a thorough discussion of certain processes in human evolution that clarify the meaning of the Evangelist's account of events preceding the Christ's incarnation. To understand what the author of the Luke Gospel tells us about the personality and ministry of Christ Jesus — that is, of the individuality who worked on for three years as the Christ in a human body — we must first sketch certain aspects of human evolution that are very difficult to grasp in our time. In many respects, we are extraordinarily short-sighted today. We think that the laws governing human evolution have always been the same as they are now — or at least as they have been for the past two or three centuries. In particular, we are convinced that laws not currently in effect never existed at all. Consequently, accounts of a past as distant as the time when the Christ lived on are very difficult for our contemporaries to understand and accept without bias.

If we are receptive to the true meaning of Luke the Evangelist's account of the Christ's deeds, we gain a better and better idea of the state of human evolution at that time. Let's briefly summarize our anthroposophical studies of modern humanity's origins in Atlantis. Our ancestors — that is, our own souls in different bodies — lived on the continent of Atlantis, which was located west of Europe and Africa and east of America. When the great Atlantean catastrophe transformed the face of the earth, throngs of human beings moved east and west away from Atlantis, populating the post-Atlantean world and founding its successive civilizations — the cultures of ancient India, ancient Persia, Egypt and Chaldea, Greece and Rome, and, ultimately, the culture we live in today.

It is totally false to assume that human beings throughout post-Atlantean times were always the same as they are today. Human nature has undergone tremendous changes. Material historical records document only a few thousand years of human history, however, and only the document we call the Akashic record, which we described briefly earlier in this lecture cycle and which is inaccessible to superficial research, provides insight into all post-Atlantean developments. In the ancient Indian or first post-Atlantean culture, human beings lived primarily in their ether bodies and did not penetrate their physical bodies as strongly as they did later. The ancient Indians did not develop modern I-consciousness, and most of them were dimly clairvoyant. Their consciousness resembled our dream consciousness, but it still reached into the spiritual worlds that underlie our existence. We tend to emphasize our ancient Indian forebears' cognitive processes, because understanding these faculties may help us move into the future. We must focus on one of their other attributes, however, if we want to understand the Luke Gospel.

In ancient India, the human ether body was much less closely connected to the physical body and extended much further beyond it on all sides than it does today. Soul forces and soul attributes affected the physical body much more strongly. The more the ether body entered the physical body, the weaker it became and the less control it exerted over the physical body. In Atlanteans, and to a certain extent even in ancient Indians, the etheric head still extended far beyond the physical body and permitted the development of both clairvoyant consciousness and a high degree of control over physical, bodily processes.

Let's consider the differences between an ancient Indian body and a modern body. Although the modern ether body has descended as deeply as possible into the physical body and has united with physical phenomena to the greatest possible extent, we are approaching a time when the ether body will begin to withdraw and become more independent of the physical body. As humankind speeds toward the future, the ether body will continue to withdraw from the physical body. Today we are slightly past the nadir of the ether body's closest association with the physical body. Compared to a modern body, the ancient Indian ether body was still relatively free of the physical body, and the Indian soul developed forces that influenced the physical body. Because it was not so closely bound to the physical body, the ether body absorbed soul forces and exerted more control over the physical body. Consequently, anything that affected the soul also affected the physical body to a very great extent. Modern ether bodies no longer have this ability.

In ancient India, a hate-filled word spoken by one person actually pierced its recipient, working right into the structure of the physical body. In contrast, a loving word had an expansive, warming effect on the recipient's soul and physical body. The soul still influenced the physical body via the ether body. At that time, the difference between a hate-filled word and a loving word was very important because words directly affected bodily processes. This effect lessened as the human ether body descended further into the physical body, and today the situation is different. Today our words initially affect only the recipient's soul, and very few people still experience a hateful or unloving word as binding and constricting or a loving word as expansive and blessing. In the early stages of post-Atlantean evolution, the unique effects of loving or hateful words, which we can still sense today in our physical hearts, were much more intense and could be manipulated very differently. How a word is spoken is no longer crucially important today. No matter how warmly a word is spoken, it more or less bounces off when it strikes a modern human constitution. The depth to which it penetrates now depends not only on how it is spoken but also on the body's ability to receive it.

Today it is impossible to work so directly on the human soul that our words also penetrate the body's physical structure. In the future such effects will become possible, however, because the spirit will regain its significance. Let me suggest briefly what this future will be like. We can accomplish very little in this regard in our present incarnation cycle because the love, goodwill, and wisdom that live in a human soul cannot pour directly into another soul where it might acquire the strength to affect the physical body. Today we know that we will only gradually learn to produce such spiritual effects. They are beginning to develop again, however, especially wherever the seeds of the spiritual scientific worldview are planted. Today, words very seldom have physical effects. Individuals can, however, come together to receive a number of spiritual truths that will gradually gain the strength required to shape the physical body in their own image. In the future, the soul-spiritual element will once again acquire a great deal of power over the physical element.

In the original Indian culture of ancient times, for example, so-called healing was different from what it would later become, as you may suspect from what we have just heard. Because anything that affected the soul also had tremendous effects on the body, a word imbued with the right will impulse could stimulate another person's soul to affect the physical body via the ether body. By exerting the right effect on another person's soul, you could work on a diseased constitution and restore health right down to the level of the physical body. Indian physicians cultivated this ability to the utmost. Above all, they mastered the necessary soul effects. We must realize that in ancient India, healing was a much more spiritual process than it can possibly be today. We are beginning to rediscover such ways of working, however. A worldview brought down from cosmic spiritual heights, a sum of truths corresponding to the great spiritual contents of the cosmos, will flow into human souls. As humankind moves toward the future, this worldview will become a means of healing that works outward from within. In the future, spiritual science will be a great remedy for human souls. We must understand, however, that humankind is now at the nadir of a descending path of evolution, that spiritual effects have increasingly receded, and that we will only gradually be able to return to the heights we once occupied.

The effects that were so prominent in ancient India were lost very slowly. A similar human constitution, which permitted one soul to affect another, still persisted in ancient Egypt. As we go further back in Egyptian culture, we discover more direct soul-to-soul effects that could then be transferred to the physical body. Such effects were much less common in ancient Persian culture, which had a different calling, namely, to provide the initial impetus for mastering the physical environment. With regard to the characteristics I just described, Egyptian culture is much closer to India than to Persia. In Persia, souls were meant to develop self-awareness and therefore became increasingly self-contained and lost control of the physical body. Thus the spiritual current that maintained the spirit's mastery over physical matter had to flow into a different culture, one that was concerned primarily with awakening self-awareness through inner contemplation. A balance between these two currents emerged in what we call Greco-Roman civilization in the fourth post-Atlantean cultural period. At that point, humankind had descended deeply enough into the physical world to establish a balance of sorts between the physical element and the soul-spiritual element. That is, in this fourth cultural period the soul and spirit controlled the body to roughly the same extent that the body controlled the soul. Humankind had descended to a state of balance.

In our time, however, humankind must first undergo a cosmic test to be able to return to spiritual heights. That is why we have descended still deeper into physical matter since Greco-Roman times. All aspects of our bodily, physical nature have continued to descend. In the fifth post-Atlantean cultural epoch, we have been driven below the balance point. At the moment, the only upward steps that are open to us are the inner steps of strengthening ourselves inwardly and cultivating a rather theoretical knowledge of the spiritual world.

In contrast to Greco-Roman culture, which represented a relatively balanced state, the physical element has gained the upper hand and dominates the soul-spiritual element in our culture. In a certain respect, the soul-spiritual element has fallen unconscious; we can absorb it only theoretically. For centuries, inner human nature has been restricted to strengthening itself in ways not apparent to manifest consciousness. Our inner aspect must gradually become stronger so we can develop a new awareness of it. In the sixth post-Atlantean cultural period, when our soul-spiritual element has achieved a certain strength, it will possess the living truth — not merely a theoretical truth — about the spiritual nourishment that we take in to an increasing extent. The spiritual will grow strong enough to master the physical body again, this time from the opposite direction.

From this perspective, how can we explain the mission of spiritual science on behalf of humanity? If spiritual science increasingly becomes a living reality in our time, warming the soul as well as stimulating human reason or intellect, the soul will grow strong enough to regain mastery over the physical element. Of course there will be transitional stages, some of which will seem regressive or even harmful, but they will eventually make way for a time when human beings will imbue their ideas with the spirit's life. In all human beings, the soul-spiritual element will master the physical, material element. Any individual who not only is interested in spiritual scientific wisdom as an intellectual stimulus but also delights in spiritual scientific truths and takes deep and vital satisfaction in them is a precursor to the souls who will once again achieve their rightful mastery over the body.

The progressive step we can take already today is to introduce great truths about mighty events such as those in Palestine just before the confluence of the Buddha and Zarathustra elements at the beginning of the Christian era. In the last few days, we described how the wisdom guiding world progress produced the Nathanic and Solomonic Jesus children and paved the way for the confluence of these cosmic currents, which had previously flowed separately.

Two views are possible about the content we absorbed in the last few days. Some people may assess it rationally and conclude that while it all seems somewhat fantastical to modern consciousness, it seems quite plausible when weighed against external events. Such people may reason that the Gospels become comprehensible only when we assume the truth of the Akashic record. They may be interested in what was said about the two Jesus figures and find that it satisfies their curiosity and explains previously inexplicable phenomena. Others may be left with an impression of the indescribable beauty of the events of cosmic evolution documented by esoteric research — of the wondrous descent of the Buddha's Nirmanakaya, the spiritual foundation of the annunciation to the shepherds; of the star that guided Zarathustra's followers to where their leader was reborn; of the confluence of cosmic currents that formerly ran separately. Learning about these events may leave us with an impression of great glory, power, and grandeur. The truth about cosmic events sets our souls afire and makes us glow with enthusiasm. Small truths satisfy our thirst for knowledge, but great truths warm our souls and reveal the immense beauty of cosmic events. When we sense their beauty and glory, knowledge begins to take root in us and to transcend mere theoretical understanding. After all, what does Christ Jesus say in the Luke Gospel?

> A sower went out to sow his seed; and as he sowed, some fell along the path, and was trodden underfoot, and the birds of the air devoured it. And some fell on the rock; and as it grew up, it withered away, because it had no moisture. And some fell among thorns, and the thorns grew with it and choked it. And some fell into good soil, and grew, and yielded a hundredfold (Luke 8:5-8).

The explanation Christ Jesus gave his disciples of the parable of the sower also applies to anthroposophy. The seed is the kingdom of the gods, the kingdom of heaven, the kingdom of the spirit, which is meant to fall like a seed into human souls. An individual's soul forces may repel the spiritual worldview, or the kingdom of divine-spiritual beings. This seed is consumed by obstacles in the human soul, is rejected immediately before it can germinate, or is eaten by birds before it works its way into the soil. Many people heard and rejected the words of Christ Jesus, and many today hear and reject anthroposophy's gift to the world. These same words, however — either the words of Christ Jesus or words of spiritual wisdom — may also be heard by souls not deep enough to receive them. Such a soul may be prepared to hear, understand,

and acknowledge the truth, and even to pass it on to others, yet remain unable to unite with it. This truth is like the seed that falls on the rocks and cannot sprout. Other seeds fall among brambles, where they sprout but cannot thrive. As Christ Jesus explained, this means that some human souls are so preoccupied with ordinary life and its cares that even though they understand the word of spiritual truth, their other soul content is like a bramble patch that hampers its growth. Many souls today cannot overcome the outer obstacles to acquiring spiritual scientific truths. Only a few can allow such truths to unfold freely, like seed that falls on good soil. These souls begin to sense the living truth of anthroposophy, absorb its living element, and dwell in it completely. Such individuals presage the future efficacy of spiritual truths. We learn to trust spiritual wisdom and become convinced of its effectiveness only through personal, inner soul strength. No outer means can convince us of its truth and power.

Spiritual wisdom still has no positive physical effects on many people today. Does this mean that it is ineffective? On the contrary, the negative effects it may have on the mighty physical bodies it encounters simply prove its inherent health. A child in poor physical health, weakened by breathing city air from infancy, may become really sick instead of healthy when exposed to clean mountain air. This does not prove that mountain air is unhealthy, nor does the fact that spiritual wisdom may cause temporary damage in certain human constitutions prove that it is harmful or ineffective. Spiritual truths encounter hundreds and thousands of years of physical heredity that is not suited to receive them.

In this context, we cannot look for proof in the outer world. We must thoroughly investigate spiritual wisdom and convince ourselves of its truth. Regardless of outer indications of its truth, we must be able to penetrate its inner aspect and develop a personal conviction. If anthroposophical wisdom sometimes seems overly aggressive, that is because it encounters unhealthy circumstances in human beings. Spiritual wisdom is perfectly healthy, but human beings are not. That is why the spiritual wisdom that will be revealed in the course of time cannot be disclosed today in its entirety and all at once. We must avoid causing excessive damage; we cannot send city children out into the mountain air that sears their lungs. It is only possible to convey as much as human beings, on the average, can bear. If still deeper wisdom were revealed, individuals with certain constitutions might collapse under the burden, just as their physical health might be disturbed in mountain air. The greatest wisdom can be disclosed to humankind only gradually. It will eventually be disclosed, however, and will become a comprehensive source of healing. These considerations underlie the so-called spiritual scientific movement.

From ancient India to Greco-Roman times, the human soul and spirit gradually lost their mastery over matter, and we must now regain it. As late as Greece and Rome, some individuals still experienced the loosening of the ether body from the physical body; consequently, their entire constitutions were receptive to soul-spiritual effects. That is why Christ Jesus appeared at that particular time. If he appeared today, he would not be able to work as he did then or to offer the same great example. In our time, he would encounter human constitutions that have descended much more deeply into physical matter and can no longer be as powerfully influenced by the soul and spirit, and he himself would have had to incarnate into such a physical constitution.

This perspective applies not only to Christ Jesus but also to similar phenomena in humankind's evolution, such as the Buddha's appearance. We saw that the Buddha's mission was to introduce the great doctrine of love, compassion, and all related virtues included in the eightfold path. Do you think that if the Buddha appeared today, he would be able to fulfil that mission in the same way? He would not. No modern human constitution would permit the Buddha to undergo developments that were still possible in his time. Human physical constitutions have continued to evolve, and the exemplary constitution that allowed the Buddha to incarnate was possible only at a very specific point in time. He used this constitution to perform a mighty deed, namely, to exemplify the eightfold path for all human beings to emulate. Today we are meant to gradually acquire the eightfold path through soul-spiritual means. This statement may sound strange, but it is really true. All our philosophical and moral accomplishments to date are only a feeble step toward achieving what the Buddha first introduced. No matter how much we may admire the philosophies of Kant and others, they are elementary and fragmentary in comparison to the comprehensive principles of the eightfold path. We will only gradually ascend to a level that allows us to understand what underlies the words of the eightfold path.

Each new element in human evolution is first introduced as a mighty deed that serves as a starting point for further evolution. A long time passes before we successfully emulate the model presented symbolically in that deed. In his own time, the Buddha introduced the doctrine of love and compassion as a sign for future generations who will gradually recognize the eightfold path in themselves. In the sixth cultural epoch, a fair number of people will be able to do this, but we have a long way to go before our souls resemble the Buddha's and we all internalize what he introduced symbolically five or six centuries before Christ.

A few contemporaries of the individual who first introduces a new element in human evolution are born with the ability to understand it, but the remaining great majority of human beings ascends slowly toward the goal and achieves it only much later. When many people have understood the eightfold path from within, rather than by hearing about it from Buddhism, a great deal will have been accomplished with regard to individual inner development. In the chapter on the effects of initiation in my book *How to Know Higher Worlds*, you can read about the relationship between the eightfold path and the sixteen-petaled lotus flower.[1] The eightfold path will enable individuals to develop the sixteen-petaled lotus flower. The two are intimately related. The sixteen-petaled lotus flower is one of the first organs that people will learn to use in the future, so for those who can survey human evolution, its degree of development indicates the extent to which humankind has evolved. Fully developing this organ establishes a certain mastery of the soul-spiritual element over the physical. Only those committed to esoteric spiritual development are truly engaged in internalizing the eightfold path. Others merely "study" it, which is also valuable as a stimulus.

As we see, the soul-spiritual element essentially becomes active only in individuals who begin to organically unite the spiritual wisdom they receive with their own souls. To the extent that the eightfold path becomes a matter of personal experience, it works back on the physical body. To be sure, clever modern materialists may tell us, for example, that they knew someone who cultivated spiritual development but died at age fifty, so the spiritual truths he brought to life in himself did little to prolong his life. What they say is quite true; this is a familiar phenomenon. It is simply unfortunate that no opposing evidence is presented. For instance, how long would the person in question have lived if he had not undergone a course of spiritual development? Perhaps he would only have lived to be forty! This issue would have to be resolved first. People always simply affirm what actually happens and disregard what would have happened otherwise, which is crucial in understanding such matters.

Within humankind, soul-spiritual mastery of the physical element receded during the fourth cultural epoch. The Christ had to appear when enough people could still demonstrate the spirit's effect on matter. If he had come later, he would not have been able to do what he did. His appearance was sorely needed, but it had to occur at the right time.

What is the significance of the Christ's incarnation? By truly understanding the Christ, we learn to exert our full self-awareness or I-consciousness. The human I learns to master all other aspects of the human being. That was the purpose of the Christ's appearance. The self-aware I will regain everything that humankind has lost through the ages. Just as the eightfold path had to be introduced by the Buddha, however, I-mastery over all external, bodily processes also had to be introduced in visible form before ancient times drew to a close. If the Christ-principle entered the world in our time, it would not have the same mighty healing effects on its surroundings. It had to appear when human ether bodies still extended far enough to receive the mighty effects of the Christ's mere word or touch. At best, only faint echoes of such effects are possible today. Along with the I, humankind began to develop an understanding of the Christ, which will become a point of departure for regaining everything humankind once lost. The few remaining receptive individuals demonstrated the powerful effects of the Christ-I on its contemporaries. At that time the I was fully present only in the Christ, but it will be present in all human beings at the end of the phase of evolution.

As the Luke Gospel shows, the Christ-I pervaded the human physical, etheric, and astral bodies so thoroughly that it exerted healing effects on the entire bodily constitutions of others. This phenomenon exemplified the strength that each human I will acquire in future millennia, when all will be able to induce effects that once emanated only from the Christ. The effects of the ideal I could be introduced to humankind only at that particular time and had to be demonstrated through many different examples.

Luke shows us examples of diseases that originate in the human astral body. How they manifest relates to the individual's entire being. In modern human beings, questionable moral qualities may be no more than soul-deep. Because modern souls do not master the body to the extent possible in the time of Christ Jesus, sins are less easily expressed as physical illnesses. But we are gradually approaching the time when the ether body will reemerge from the physical body, when we will have to prevent moral and intellectual vices from manifesting in physical illness. This time is already beginning, as indicated by many modern nervous disorders, which are half psychological and half physical. When our thinking and perceptions absorb unharmonious aspects of our environment, the natural consequences are symptoms such as hysteria. These symptoms, however, relate to the unique quality of the spiritual evolution that we are beginning to undergo, namely, the reemergence of the ether body.

When the Christ appeared, he encountered many people whose illnesses expressed their sins, that is, character defects based on unfortunate traits in earlier incarnations. In the Luke Gospel, a defect in the astral body that appears as an illness is called "possession," which means that foreign spirits enter the astral body of an individual whose better qualities do not maintain mastery over his or her full humanity. In the many human beings who still experienced the old separation of the ether body from the physical body, negative character traits frequently manifested as possession. The Luke Gospel gives examples of people healed by the touch and word of the Christ individuality, who drove out the evil in them. The Christ presented an example of the healing effects that positive qualities will exert by the end of evolution.

We usually do not notice the subtle differences in these healings that suggest the different type of illness involved. An example of this is the healing of the "palsied" man (Luke 5:17–26), which should actually be called the healing of the paralytic, because the Greek text uses the word *paralelyménos*, which means someone whose limbs are paralyzed. In those times, people still knew that such illnesses originated in characteristics of the ether body. That Christ Jesus healed people who were paralyzed tells us that the forces of his individuality affected not only astral bodies but also ether bodies, so that individuals with defective ether bodies could also experience his healing influence. The words the Christ uses to indicate deep-seated sin in the ether body are noteworthy. The spiritual element that causes sickness must be banished first, so the Christ, instead of immediately telling the sick man to get up and walk, first addresses the cause, which works right down into the ether body. He says, "Your sins are forgiven you"; that is, the sins that have eaten their way into your ether body must be eliminated first. Ordinary Bible scholarship does not pursue these finer distinctions and thus fails to recognize that the individuality of the Christ influenced the mysteries of both the astral body and the ether body, and even the mysteries of the physical body itself.

Why does this chapter seem to speak of the mysteries of the physical body as uppermost, when even in our physical existence the effect of one astral body on another is the most readily apparent? When you hurt someone with a hate-filled word, a process is triggered in the recipient's astral body, where the offending word is experienced as suffering. This is an example of an exchange between astral bodies. Exchanges between etheric bodies are much more hidden and involve more subtle interpersonal effects that are generally disregarded today. Effects on the physical body are the most heavily concealed, however, because dense matter effectively insulates the physical body from spiritual effects. However, we are also meant to see that Christ Jesus mastered the physical body. How does he demonstrate his mastery? At this point, we open a chapter that will be totally incomprehensible to modern materialistic thinkers. Fortunately, all of you are knowledgeable about spiritual science. To anyone coming in from the street, what we are discussing today would sound totally insane, even if only half or a quarter of the previous lectures sounded crazy.

Christ Jesus demonstrated his ability to understand and influence human physical, bodily nature. His strength cured diseases rooted in the physical body. To understand this, we must be aware of the mysterious effects that work from one physical body to another to alleviate physical illness. When spiritual effects come into play, we cannot consider the human being as confined within the skin. We have often said that each one of our fingers is wiser than we are. Blood flows through a finger only because it flows through the entire body in the right way, and a finger knows that it will atrophy if separated from the rest of the body. If we truly understood the situation in our body, we would know that the physical body belongs to humankind as a whole, that effects constantly pass from one physical body to the other, and that we cannot separate the health of a single human being from the health of humankind as a whole. Today we acknowledge the truth of this statement with regard to crude effects but not with regard to more subtle effects, because we cannot know the real situation. The Luke Gospel, however, points out these more subtle effects. Chapter 8 tells of events leading up to the curing of the twelve-year-old daughter of Jairus:

> Now when Jesus returned, the crowd welcomed him, for they were all waiting for him. And there came a man named Jairus, who was a ruler of the synagogue; and falling at Jesus' feet he besought him to come to his house, for he had an only daughter, about twelve years of age, and she was dying. As he went the people pressed round him. And a woman who had had a flow of blood for twelve years, and could not be healed by anyone, came up behind him, and touched the fringe of his garment; and immediately her flow of blood ceased (Luke 8:40-44).

How could the girl be cured if she was dying? To understand this, we must know that her physical illness was related to another person's symptoms and could not be cured without taking them into account. The girl, now twelve, was born with a deep karmic connection to another personality. We are told that a woman who had suffered from her particular disorder for twelve years approached the Christ from behind and touched the hem of his garment. This woman is mentioned here because she was karmically linked to Jairus's daughter. It is no coincidence that the girl was dying at age twelve and that the woman had been sick for twelve years. Their conditions are related. The woman approached Jesus and was cured. Only then could he enter Jairus's house and cure his daughter, who was already presumed dead. Grasping the karma that weaves between individuals requires a very profound perspective. In this example, we can see the Christ's third means of working — namely, on the entire human constitution. We must keep it in mind as the Luke Gospel reveals the Christ's higher activity.

The Luke Gospel illustrates how the I-being of the Christ influenced all other members of the human constitution. This is the important aspect of these accounts. The author of the Luke Gospel emphasized healing effects and attempted to show how they reveal an I at the pinnacle of human evolution. He shows the inevitable effects of the Christ on the human astral body, ether body, and physical body. Luke introduced the great model for our future evolution, telling us that the human I, still weak today, will gradually master and transform the astral body, the ether body, and the physical body. The Christ appeared as the great ideal to which humankind must aspire. He shows us the results of the I's mastery over the other members of the human constitution.

Such are the truths underlying the Gospels, which are based not on other documents but on the testimony of "independent seers" and "servants of the word." Only gradually will humanity grow convinced of what lies behind the Gospels. Then, with a strength and intensity that will truly affect all other members of the human constitution, we will progressively internalize the Scriptures' substance.

BASEL, SEPTEMBER 24, 1909

NOTE

1. Rudolf Steiner, *How to Know Higher Worlds: A Modern Path of Initiation*. Hudson, N.Y.: Anthroposophic Press, 1994.

NINE

Christ and Maitreya Buddha

As you will have gathered from yesterday's lecture, we can understand a document like the Luke Gospel only by applying the higher perspective supplied by spiritual science to the evolution of the entire human constitution. To understand the Luke Gospel, we must first understand the radical change that occurred in humankind at the time of Christ Jesus. It will be helpful to compare this change to one that is taking place in our own time. This latter change, although more gradual, is clearly evident, but to understand it, we must abandon a very prevalent and comfortable bias, namely, that no great leaps occur in nature or in evolution. From the ordinary perspective, there is nothing more false than this statement. Nature constantly takes leaps; leaps are the very essence of development. For example, let's look at how a seed sprouts. The emergence of the first leaf constitutes a significant leap forward. Another leap occurs in the transition from leaf to flower, another in the transition from the outer to the inner parts of the flower, and another, very significant leap occurs when the fruit develops. We cannot understand nature if we fail to consider such leaps. Having observed evolution progressing at a snail's pace in one century, we would be mistaken to assume that the rate of change will always remain the same. At certain times, evolution may proceed slowly, as when a plant moves from one green leaf to the next. A leap occurs in the plant, however, when the last leaf has emerged and flower buds begin to form, and comparable repeated leaps occur in the evolution of the human race.

One such significant leap occurred at the time when Christ Jesus appeared. In a relatively short time, the properties of ancient clairvoyance and the spirit's mastery over the bodily element were transformed and nearly eliminated. Before this transition occurred, the legacy of ancient times asserted itself one final time. This was the context of Christ Jesus' work, which enabled humankind to absorb a new element and slowly, gradually evolve further.

In a different domain, a leap is also occurring now. Although more gradual, it is quite comprehensible to those who want to understand our time. We can best gain an idea of this change by listening to people who approach spiritual science from different spiritual perspectives. Not infrequently, for example, members of various religious denominations attend lectures on spiritual science. What I am going to say next is completely understandable and is not intended as a reproach. When these people attend spiritual scientific lectures on the nature of Christianity, their response is often, "That's all well and good, and it doesn't really contradict anything we hear from the pulpit, but we say it in ways that everyone can understand. In contrast, what we just heard is understandable to only a few." This very common response implies that their view of Christianity is the only view. Such people disregard a universal obligation to judge on the basis of facts rather than personal preference. I once had to say to such a person, "You may believe that you proclaim Christian truths to all people. However, this issue is decided by the facts, not by your belief. Does everyone attend your church? The facts demonstrate the opposite! Spiritual science is not there for those for whom your approach is adequate; it is there for those who need something different."[1] We must judge on the basis of facts rather than personal preference, and as a general rule it is very difficult for people to distinguish their preferences from fact.

What would happen if such people persisted in believing that their approach is right for all and continued to harangue all who speak differently? Would spiritual life survive at all? An increasing number of people would no longer be able to hear spiritual facts proclaimed in traditional ways. Fewer and fewer people would even bother to listen to such proclamations. And if there were no spiritual scientific movement, these people would have nothing to satisfy their spiritual needs and would fade away for lack of nourishment. How to present spiritual nourishment is no longer a matter of individual choice but a matter for evolution to determine. In our current time and situation, people's spiritual needs with regard to interpreting the Gospels and so on must be satisfied. How we choose to provide spiritual nourishment, however, is not the point. The point is how human souls ask for it. Today, their longing for spiritual science is evident. Whether those who choose to teach in other ways will be able to meet the spiritual needs of our time is no longer up to them; they will simply find themselves with ever fewer listeners.

In our time, it is becoming ever less possible for human hearts to accept the Bible as it was accepted in the past four or five centuries of Western cultural history. Either humankind will receive spiritual science and learn to understand the Bible in new ways, or nonanthroposophists will no longer be able to listen to the Bible. In the latter case, humankind will lose the Bible completely. It will disappear, and with it the greatest spiritual treasures of earthly evolution. We are facing an evolutionary leap. Human hearts are asking for a spiritual scientific explanation of the Bible. If they get it, the blessings of the Bible will be preserved for humankind; if not, the Bible will be lost. People who believe that their preferences and their traditional way of reading the Bible absolutely must be preserved will have to accept this state of affairs and the leap that we can take in our time. If we recognize this leap, we also acknowledge the spiritual scientific movement as a necessity in human evolution and will not be dissuaded from cultivating anthroposophy.

From a higher perspective, the leap that is occurring now is relatively small compared to the one that occurred when Christ Jesus appeared on earth. At that time humankind was in the last throes of an evolutionary phase begun in ancient times — in fact, in the earth's previous embodiment. Throughout that entire time, most of human evolution involved the physical, etheric, and astral bodies. The I, although it had since been part of the human constitution, still played a subordinate role. Until Christ Jesus appeared, the completely self-aware human I was still overshadowed by its three protective coverings.

What would have happened if Christ Jesus had not come to earth? Human evolution would have progressed until the I emerged fully, but as the I emerged, all the earlier outstanding capabilities of the astral, etheric, and physical bodies would have disappeared. All ancient clairvoyance, all mastery of soul and spirit over the body, would have had to disappear. The human being would have become an increasingly self-aware but increasingly egotistical I, and all the love on earth would have died out. It is essential to note this point.

At the time of Christ Jesus, humankind was ready to develop the I, or self, but had transcended old forms of influence from outside. In ancient Hebrew culture, for example, the law proclaimed from Mount Sinai was effective because the I had not yet fully emerged; the astral body, as the highest fully present member, was receptive to having appropriate behaviors and feelings imbued or imprinted from outside. For the last time before the I's full emergence, the law streamed into human beings from outside. If the I had emerged and nothing else had happened, human beings would have focused exclusively on the I. Although humankind was ready for I-development, the I would have become empty, thinking only of itself and wanting to do nothing for other people or for the wider world.

Christ's deed on earth was to provide content for the I, to inspire the I to learn to overflow with the power of love. Without the Christ, the I would have been an empty vessel; through his appearance, it is increasingly filled with love. That is why the Christ said to those around him, When you see clouds gathering, you know a storm is coming. You judge the weather on the basis of physical signs, but you do not understand the signs of the times. (Luke 12:54–59) If you understood them and were able to judge what happens around you, you would know that the divinity must pervade and impregnate the I, and you would not say that you can continue to live with what has come down from the past. The scribes and Pharisees offer you an outdated legacy and want to add nothing to it. Their leaven, however, will no longer work in human evolution. Those who choose to abide by Moses and the Prophets do not understand the signs of the times and do not recognize the transition occurring in humankind. In significant words, Christ Jesus told those around him that being Christian is not a matter of personal preference but a necessity for human progress. In the speeches preserved in the Luke Gospel about the "signs of the time" and about the inadequacy of the "old leaven" of the scribes and Pharisees, who wanted only to preserve the old ways, the Christ explains that the old leaven seems adequate only to those who judge exclusively on the basis of personal preference and feel no obligation to judge according to the necessities of world evolution that he was teaching. For this reason, the Christ called the aim of the scribes and Pharisees an "untruth" in the sense of something that no longer corresponds to the outer world.

We can best sense the emotional power of his speech by comparing it to corresponding processes in our time. How would it sound if what the Christ Jesus said about the scribes and Pharisees were transposed to our time? Are there people today who are like the scribes? Indeed there are. They choose not to participate in a deeper explanation of the Gospels, to go no further than what faculties acquired without benefit of spiritual science tell them about the Gospels. They do not want to move toward understanding the depths of the Gospels as spiritual science teaches us to do. This resistance is basically the same wherever people attempt to interpret the Gospels, whether in progressive or regressive ways. The ability to interpret the Gospels emerges only from spiritual science. Because spiritual science alone can help us learn the truth about the Gospels, all other scriptural research seems futile and leaves real truth-seekers cold. Today, however, we must add to the scribes and Pharisees a third category of people, the natural scientists, who reject all the acquired faculties that enable us to research the spiritual foundations of natural phenomena. Today when we speak as Christ Jesus might have spoken, we confront academics whose function is to categorize natural phenomena. They reject all spiritual explanations and hamper the progress of human evolution by refusing to recognize the signs of the times in the sense described above.

Christ Jesus found the courage to speak out against those who acknowledged only Moses and the Prophets. In our time, following in his footsteps would entail finding the courage — as he found the courage to speak out against those who acknowledged only Moses and the prophets — to speak out against all those who want to turn back the clock on human progress by opposing anthroposophical interpretation of both the Scriptures and natural phenomena. The well-intentioned few who make vague attempts to keep the peace should take to heart what Christ Jesus says in the Luke Gospel about the impossibility of serving two masters.

Among the most beautiful and compelling parables in the Luke Gospel is the one usually called the parable of the unjust steward (Luke 16:1–13). It tells of a rich man who decided to dismiss a steward who was rumored to be squandering his fortune. The steward was extremely perturbed and wondered what to do next, since he did not know how to work the land and was too ashamed to beg. Then he thought of a way out of his predicament. He realized that his business associates did not like him because he had consistently put his master's interest above theirs in all his dealings with them. To avoid absolute ruin, he had to gain their favor and demonstrate his goodwill. So he went to one of his master's debtors, asked how much he owed, and allowed him to write off half of the debt. He did the same thing with all the others, seeking to gain their goodwill so that when his master dismissed him he could turn to them and would not have to starve. Such was his reasoning. Then the Gospel says something that may astonish some readers: "The master commended the dishonest steward for his shrewdness." Some modern interpreters of the Gospel expressed doubt about who this "master" might be, even though it is quite clear that Jesus himself praised the steward's shrewdness. The Gospel continues, "for the children of this world are in their generation wiser than the children of light" (Luke 16:8). These words have stood there in the Bible for hundreds of years. Why has no one questioned the meaning of this verse? "In their generation" appears in all the different translations of the Bible, but the correct translation of the Greek text is "for the children of this world are wiser *in their own way* than the children of light." In other words, according to their own understanding of the situation, the children of this world are wiser. For centuries, all the translators mistranslated "in their own way" because the Greek phrase *ten genean* sounds very similar to the Greek word for "generation" and is even used in that sense in some cases. How can an error like this persist for centuries? Even Weizäcker, a recent translator who reputedly went to great lengths to recreate the correct wording, goes along with it. Strangely enough, people seem to forget all their education when they try to establish authoritative versions of the Scriptures.

Above all, the spiritual scientific worldview will give us back the Bible as it really is. The Bible we have today is not the real Bible, and we cannot imagine what the books of the Bible are really like. Their most important passages are not accurate, as I will now demonstrate in greater detail. The intended meaning of the parable of the unjust steward is clearly stated in the Luke Gospel. The steward, reflecting on his imminent dismissal, realized that he had to win favor among people and that he could not serve two masters. The Christ then tells his listeners that they, too, cannot serve two masters; they cannot serve both the God who is trying to win their hearts and the god proclaimed by the scribes and the interpreters of the Prophets. We cannot serve both the Christ-principle, which is working to bring human evolution a step forward, and the god who attempts to obstruct progressive evolution. When it persists into later times, everything that was right in times past eventually becomes an obstacle to later evolution. This is a basic premise of evolution. In Jesus' time, "Mammon" was a technical term for the powers of obstruction. You cannot serve both the God of progress and Mammon, the god of obstruction. The steward, that "child of this world," realized that even Mammon does not allow one to serve two masters, and those who aspire to becoming "children of light" must also realize that they cannot serve two masters.

How can we clothe this parable in Christian terms appropriate to our time? Modern human beings must realize that no compromise is possible between the modern Mammon —

that is, traditional scholars and scientists — and the current that must provide nourishment for humankind.

Our understanding of the Gospels must come alive, as must spiritual science itself. Everything spiritual science touches must come to life, and the Gospels must fructify our spiritual faculties. Simply talking about Christ Jesus' repudiation of the scribes and Pharisees is not enough, because by doing so we refer again to a time that is now past. We must enliven our understanding by learning to recognize the contemporary, living manifestations and successors of what Christ Jesus, using the vocabulary of his time, called Mammon. Both our recognition of the contemporary Mammon and the parable of the steward, which is told only in the Luke Gospel, relate to one of the most important concepts in the Gospels. We can understand this concept with heart, soul, and mind only by considering the Buddha's impact on Christ Jesus from a different perspective.

We said that the Buddha introduced the great doctrine of compassion and love to humankind. In cases like this, esoteric statements must be taken very precisely. Otherwise, someone might say that I contradicted myself by saying on one occasion that the Christ brought love to earth and on another that the Buddha brought the doctrine of love. But are these two statements the same? In one instance, I said that the Buddha brought the doctrine of love to earth and in the other that the Christ brought the living power of love to earth. There is a big difference between these statements. When humankind's most profound concerns are involved, we must listen very carefully, because otherwise people compare statements made on different occasions and then say that I postulated two proclaimers of love in order to satisfy everyone. In esotericism, exact listening is important. When we truly understand the significant truths clothed in these words, we will see them in the right light.

We know that the eightfold path completely encompasses all of the Buddha's great doctrine of compassion and love. What is the goal or destination of this path? When individuals commit themselves from the depths of their souls to the ideal of the eightfold path, they begin to explore what they need to do to become as perfect as possible, to cleanse and purify the I to the greatest possible extent and to allow it to find its right place in the world. The aim of the eightfold path is to purify and ennoble the I, which is perfected by fully observing the path's precepts. As the I works to perfect itself, the individual incorporates everything that emanates from this wondrous path. This is the most essential aspect of the eightfold path. If humankind continues to cultivate what the Buddha, using a technical term, called "rolling the wheel of the law," each of us will gradually perfect our own I and learn to recognize the most perfect I-beings by their thoughts and wisdom. The Buddha gave humankind knowledge of love and compassion, and when we have completely transformed our astral bodies through the eightfold path, we will know everything we need to know about the law of this path.

There is a difference, however, between wisdom, knowledge, or thoughts and an active, living force. There is a difference between knowing what an I should be like and imbuing ourselves with a living force that can then flow from the I into the entire world, as the force emanating from the Christ influenced the astral, etheric, and physical bodies of those around him. Humankind learned the content of the doctrine of compassion and love through the contribution of the great Buddha. In contrast, the Christ's contribution is not a doctrine but a living force. He sacrificed himself and descended to earth to pervade not only the astral body but also the I, teaching it to exude the substance of love. The Christ brought to earth love's substantial, living content, not merely its wise content. This is the essence of his mission.

The great Buddha lived on earth approximately two thousand five hundred years ago. As esoteric facts teach us, the Earth phase of evolution will last for approximately another three thousand years. At that time, large numbers of people will have discovered and followed the eightfold path, the Buddha's wisdom, in their own hearts and souls. The Buddha's life on earth served as a starting point for the force that human beings would gradually develop as knowledge of the eightfold path. In approximately three thousand years, human beings will internalize it fully. Individuals will no longer receive the Buddha's teachings from outside but will discover them within themselves, allowing the eightfold path to grow and emerge as the wisdom of compassion and love.

Even if nothing further had happened after the great Buddha set the "wheel of the law" in motion, humankind would still acquire knowledge of the doctrine of compassion and love in the next three thousand years. There is a difference, however, between knowing about this doctrine and acquiring the strength to embody it and live it. There is a difference between knowing about compassion and love and developing the corresponding power under the influence of the Christ individuality, who poured love into human beings. This love will continue to grow. Thanks to the Buddha, when this phase of our evolution is complete, we will have the wisdom to recognize the content of the doctrine of compassion and love.

Thanks to the Christ, we will have learned to allow love to flow from the individual I to all humankind.

Described in this way, the interaction of the Christ and the Buddha makes the Luke Gospel understandable. We encounter their interaction as soon as we learn to correctly interpret the words of Luke 2:13–14. Down below are the shepherds, hurrying to receive the proclamation; above them is the heavenly host, the spiritual, imaginative expression of the Buddha's Nirmanakaya. Divine wisdom is revealed from the heights by the Buddha's Nirmanakaya, which hovers over the Nathanic infant Jesus in the form of the angelic host. Something else, however, is added to this revelation — "peace to human beings on earth below who are imbued with goodwill," that is, to human beings in whom the true, living force of love begins to grow. This state of "peace on earth" will be realized through the impetus the Christ provided. To the revelation from the heights, he added a living force that flowed into every human heart, where it can increase to the point of overflowing. The Christ provided no mere doctrine to be absorbed in the form of thoughts and ideas but a force that will flow from human souls. The Luke Gospel and the other Gospels consistently describe the Christ force that works in human souls as the force of faith. That is the meaning of faith in the Gospels. Those who receive the Christ and allow him to dwell in them have faith. The human I, which would otherwise be an empty vessel, fills to overflowing with love.

The Christ was able to provide such a great example of "healing through words" because he was the first to set the "wheel of love" — not the "wheel of the law" — in motion as an independent faculty and power of the human soul, because he was so filled with love that it spilled over, healing those around him, and because the words he spoke — whether "Rise and walk!" or "Your sins are forgiven you" — emerged from the abundant love overflowing within him, from an excess of love that an I could not contain. When the Christ spoke of believers, he meant anyone who internalized the reality of this love to even a slight extent. This is the only meaning we must associate with the term "faith," which is one of the most significant in the New Testament. Faith is the ability to transcend oneself, to go beyond what the I does for the sake of its own perfection. Thus, once the Christ had incarnated into the body of the Nathanic Jesus, where he united with the power of the Buddha, his teachings did not answer the question, "How is the I to become as perfect as possible?" but rather "How shall the I overflow? How can it transcend itself?" He often answered in simple words, and indeed the words of the Luke Gospel speak to the simplest hearts: It is not enough to give to those who will give back to you, for even sinners do that. If they know that they will get back what they have given, they do not give out of overflowing love. But when you give and know that you will not receive in return, you have acted out of real love (Luke 6:33–34). This love is not contained by the I, but flows freely from it. In many different variations on these words, the Christ described how the I is meant to overflow, working in the world through its excess, through self-transcendent feeling.

The warmest words in the Luke Gospel speak of overflowing love. The Luke Gospel contains a force of overflowing love that permeates our own words with its strength so that they can affect the outer world. One of the other Evangelists, whose prior experience did not allow him to emphasize overflowing love to the same extent, at least briefly summed up this Christian mystery, saying that love flows from the over-fullness of the I. Of course it must also flow into all our words and deeds. The Latin translation of the Matthew Gospel still contains authentic, original wording that briefly summarizes the Luke Gospel's beautiful praise of love: *ex abundantia cordis os loquitur,* "out of the abundance of the heart the mouth speaks" (Luke 6:45, Matt. 12:34). One of the highest Christian ideals! The mouth speaks out of the heart's abundance, out of the fullness that the heart cannot contain. The heart is moved by blood, and blood is the expression of the I. Thus this sentence means, "Speak from an overflowing I that radiates strength, for this strength is the power of faith." Then your words truly contain the power of the Christ. "The mouth speaks out of the heart's abundance" is a cardinal statement of the essence of Christianity.

And now read the same sentence in the modern [German] Bible: "Whose heart is full, his mouth shall overflow." These words have sufficed for centuries to conceal one of the cardinal principles of Christianity. Humankind has never recognized what nonsense it is to say that a full heart pours itself out. In the ordinary world, things spill only when they are more than full, when they overflow. Of necessity — and this is not meant as criticism — humankind has been caught up in an idea that completely conceals one of the most important precepts of Christianity, without even noticing that it is replaced by a sheer impossibility. If our language will not tolerate translating *ex abundantia cordis os loquitur* as "the mouth speaks out of the heart's overfullness," then we also cannot say that the overflow from a masonry stove heats the room, which is sheer nonsense. If you heat a stove only until the warmth reaches its walls, it does not warm the room. The room is warmed only when warmth exceeds the stove's capacity to contain it. This is an important issue. Part of the Luke Gospel is based on a cardinal Christian precept that has been covered up. At an important point, we cannot see what the Gospel says.

The force that overflows from the human heart — which in this context means the human I — is the power of the Christ. The I creates an excess that cannot be contained and flows out through the word. Only at the end of the Earth phase of evolution will the I fully incorporate the Christ. Meanwhile, the Christ is what overflows from human hearts. If our hearts are merely full, we do not incorporate the Christ. That is why Christianity is covered up when the full earnestness and dignity of this verse are not understood. The most important aspect of Christianity, its very essence, appears correctly when spiritual science explains lofty Christian documents. Through reading the Akashic record in the spiritual world, spiritual science uncovers the original meaning of such documents and is therefore able to read the truth in them.

Now we understand how humankind moves toward the future. The bodhisattva who became the Buddha five or six centuries before Christ ascended into the spiritual world to work through a Nirmanakaya. By doing so, he rose to a higher level. He no longer needed to descend into a physical body and now works in other ways. When he became the Buddha, he passed the office of bodhisattva to a different being who was to be his successor. Esoteric Christianity recognizes the profound truth of the Buddhist legend that tells how the bodhisattva being, before descending into incarnation as the Buddha, took off the heavenly diadem and placed it on the head of the next bodhisattva, who will continue their common efforts but with a somewhat different mission. He too is destined to become a buddha. Approximately three thousand years from now, when a number of people have discovered and followed the eightfold path out of their own resources, the bodhisattva who succeeded the Buddha will also become a buddha. This bodhisattva was entrusted with his mission five or six hundred years before the beginning of our era and will become a buddha approximately three thousand years from now. Oriental teachings call this being the Maitreya Buddha. Before the present bodhisattva can become the Maitreya Buddha, a large number of human beings must have discovered the teaching of the eightfold path in their own hearts. By then, many people will be wise enough to do so. At that time, the present bodhisattva will introduce a new force into the world.

If nothing else happened in the intervening time, the bodhisattva would still find individuals capable of discovering the teaching of the eightfold path through inner meditation, but he would not find individuals whose souls overflow with the living force of love. In the interim, this living force of love must stream in so that the Maitreya Buddha finds individuals who not only know what love is but also incorporate the power of love itself. To this end, the Christ had to descend to earth. He spent only three years on earth and had not incarnated previously, as you can gather from all of my earlier explanations. The Christ's three-year presence on earth, from the baptism in the Jordan to the mystery of Golgotha, will cause love to flow into human hearts and souls on earth — in other words, into the human I — to an ever-increasing extent. Human beings will become increasingly imbued with the Christ until, at the end of the Earth phase of evolution, he totally fills the human I. Just as the doctrine of compassion and love first had to be stimulated by the Buddha, the substance of love had to be brought to earth from heavenly heights by a being who would gradually transform it into the personal possession of each human I. It is not correct to say that love did not exist previously, but earlier love could not be the direct and personal possession of the human I. Earlier love was inspired love, love sent down from cosmic heights by the Christ. It flowed into human beings as unconsciously as the teachings of the eightfold path flowed from the bodhisattva before he became the Buddha. The Buddha embodied the eightfold path as the Christ being embodied the previously undescended Christ essence. It is essential to note that for the Christ, assuming human form was a progressive step.

The Buddha's successor, who is now a bodhisattva and will become the Maitreya Buddha, is well known to those familiar with spiritual science. In time, it will become possible to identify this bodhisattva by name. For now, however, having stated so many facts that are unknown to the outer world, we can only say that he exists. When he appears on earth as the Maitreya Buddha, he will encounter the Christ's seeds — that is, human beings whose heads are not only full of the wisdom of the eightfold path and with teachings of love but whose hearts are full of the living substance of love that overflows and streams out into the world. Together with these individuals, the Maitreya Buddha will then accomplish his further mission as cosmic evolution continues.

We must understand such relationships in order to understand the profundity of the Luke Gospel. This Gospel does not tell us about doctrines; it tells of the being who imbued earthly existence and human constitutions with his own substance. Esotericism expresses this fact by saying that the bodhisattvas, who become buddhas, save the human spirit through their wisdom but can never save the entire human being. To save the entire human being, not only wisdom but also the warm power of love must flood the entire human constitution. Christ's task was to save souls through the flood of love he brought to earth. We must distinguish between the task of the bodhisattva and Buddha, which was to introduce humankind to the wisdom or knowledge of love, and the task of the Christ, which was to introduce the power of love.

BASEL, SEPTEMBER 25, 1909

NOTE

1. This encounter occurred after a lecture Rudolf Steiner gave in Colmar on November 21, 1905. No transcript exists of this lecture, which was entitled *Die Weisheitslehren des Christentums im Lichte der Theosophie* ("The Wisdom of Christian Teachings in the Light of Theosophy"). See also Rudolf Steiner's lecture in Stuttgart on March 5, 1920, which is included in: *Polarities in the Evolution of Mankind: West and East; Materialism and Mysticism; Knowledge and Belief.* London: Rudolf Steiner Press/New York: Anthroposophic Press, 1987 (GA 197, *Gegensätze in der Menschheitsentwickelung*).

TEN

✦

The Mystery of Golgotha
as a New Form of Initiation

TODAY WE WILL SEE HOW the insights we have gained here lead us to the so-called mystery of Golgotha, which is revealed by spiritual research into the Luke Gospel. Yesterday we attempted to vividly depict what was happening in the evolution of the human race during the Christ's three years on earth, while previous lectures showed how the confluence of several spiritual currents allowed this mysterious event to occur. Insights gained from the Akashic record reveal the full value of Gospel accounts, especially of Luke the Evangelist's description of the Christ's earthly mission.

At this point, a question may arise. If in fact the Buddhist spiritual current was organically interwoven with Christianity, why is there no sign in Christian teachings of the great law of karma, of the compensation that occurs over several incarnations of the same individuality? We would be mistaken to believe that the Luke Gospel does not include insights based on the law of karma. We must realize, however, that the needs of the human soul change in the course of history. The great missionaries of world evolution, who must meet these needs in any given epoch, cannot simply promulgate absolute truths in abstract forms that would be incomprehensible to their contemporaries at that level of maturity. The great Buddha's incisive gift to humankind included insights that lead, when combined with the eightfold path's doctrine of compassion and love, to an understanding of the doctrine of karma. We cannot expect to find this understanding in human souls who have not had time to develop it.

We heard yesterday that in three thousand years a large percentage of human beings will be sufficiently advanced to discover the eightfold path within themselves. Today we can add that these individuals will also discover, albeit very gradually, the truths of reincarnation and karma. When a seed first sprouts, flowers do not develop immediately but only after the leaves emerge in lawful succession. Similarly, spiritual evolution moves through different levels in human history, and each successive phenomenon occurs at the right time. Today, the faculties we achieve through spiritual science allow us to discover the unavoidable truths of reincarnation and karma by meditating on our own souls. Earlier stages in the evolution of the human soul were not fruitless but produced the level of maturity necessary for this step. It would have been pointless to proclaim the doctrine of reincarnation and karma exoterically several centuries ago. Today, human souls long for the contents of modern spiritual science and the results of its research into the foundations of the Gospels, but the evolution of the human race would not have been advanced by publicizing these contents several hundred years ago. Before they could be presented, human souls had to hunger for them. Experiences in earlier pre-Christian and Christian incarnations developed the faculties needed to absorb the truths of karma and reincarnation. In the context of the evolution of the human race, proclaiming these truths as openly in the first centuries of Christianity as we do today would have been like asking a plant to produce flowers before it develops leaves.

Humankind has only recently matured sufficiently to begin absorbing the spiritual truths of karma and reincarnation. It is not surprising, therefore, that some passages in the Gospels have survived in forms that actually give a false picture of Christianity. In some respects, the Gospels were given to humankind prematurely, and we are only now developing the faculties that allow us to understand their true meaning. The coming of Christ Jesus had to be proclaimed in ways that respected the human soul constitution typical at that time. Reincarnation and karma could not be taught abstractly but only by imbuing human souls with feelings that allowed them to develop the necessary maturity to absorb these truths. In other words, reincarnation and karma could not be taught directly at that time. The most that could be done was to plant the seed of future understanding.

Is that what Christ Jesus and his followers said? Let's open the Luke Gospel and allow their words to flow into our souls. If we do so with the right insight, we will see how they introduced the law of karma.

> Blessed are you poor, for yours is the kingdom of God.
> Blessed are you that hunger now, for you shall be satisfied.

Blessed are you that weep now, for you shall laugh. Blessed are you when men hate you, and when they exclude you and revile you, and cast out your name as evil, on account of the Son of man! Rejoice in that day; and leap for joy, for behold, your reward is great in heaven (Luke 6:20–23).

Stated in this way, the law of compensation, instead of referring abstractly to reincarnation and karma, imbued human souls with the certainty that those who hunger will be compensated. Such feelings had to flow into human souls who would achieve the maturity needed to understand karma and reincarnation only in subsequent incarnations. Souls of that time had to receive a content that would mature in them later. A new age had arrived, a time when the human race was mature enough to begin to develop the I, or self-awareness. Previously, human beings had experienced the effects of revelations in their astral, etheric, and physical bodies, but now the I was to become fully conscious, although it would only gradually be filled with the forces it was to receive. At that time, only a single I on earth — the I of the Nathanic Jesus, whose physical nature had been prepared to embody the individuality of Zarathustra — was able to fully incorporate the all-encompassing Christ principle into an earthly personality. Now others, by emulating the Christ, must gradually incorporate this principle, which was once present in an earthly human being for three years. Christ Jesus provided no more than a stimulus for humankind; he planted a seed that must now gradually sprout and grow.

The Christ also ensured that at appropriate intervals in human evolution, individuals appeared to supply elements that others would only later be able to develop independently.

The being who walked the earth as the Christ had to ensure not only the immediate proclamation of his incarnation in ways that his contemporaries understood but also the later appearance of individuals who would provide spiritual care for maturing souls.

The author of the John Gospel describes the Christ's provisions for the times following the event of Golgotha. The Christ resurrected the individuality of John the Baptist in Lazarus to continue John's work of spreading the Christ's teachings in the form I described in lectures on the John Gospel.[1] And to ensure the later coming of another individuality[2] who would provide the maturing human race with a necessary element, the Christ had to perform a second resurrection. This awakening from the dead is faithfully described by the author of the Luke Gospel, whose stated intent was to describe what imaginative and inspired clairvoyants knew about the event of Palestine. The resurrection of the young man of Nain (Luke 7:11–17) contains the mystery of the continued effects of Christianity. The mysteries associated with the healing of Jairus's daughter, which I explained at least partially the day before yesterday, were so profound that Christ Jesus took only a few people with him to witness the healing and then told them not to talk about it. In contrast, the story of the resurrection of the young man of Nain was publicized immediately. The former was an instance of healing that resulted from a profound understanding of the physical body's processes, while the latter was an awakening or initiation. The individuality who inhabited the body of the young man of Nain was destined to experience a very specific type of initiation.

In one type of initiation, the higher worlds are illumined for the person in question as soon as the initiation process is completed, and the new initiate is immediately able to understand spiritual laws and processes. A different type of initiation merely plants a seed in the soul of the candidate, who becomes an initiate only when the seed begins to develop in a subsequent incarnation. The young man of Nain underwent the latter type of initiation. His soul, transformed during the event of Palestine, was not yet conscious of ascending into higher worlds. The forces implanted in his soul germinated only in his next incarnation. In an exoteric lecture I cannot identify this individuality by name, but I can say that these forces made him a great religious teacher in a later life. Thus the Christ ensured the later appearance of an individuality who would advance Christianity. The individuality resurrected in the young man of Nain was charged with introducing the teachings of reincarnation and karma into Christianity at a later time. When the Christ walked the earth, these truths could not be proclaimed directly because a feeling for them first had to be implanted in human souls.

In the Luke Gospel's account of his life, Christ Jesus clearly indicates that the new element of I-consciousness has entered human evolution. We must simply understand what we read. The Christ tells us that in earlier times, the spiritual world did not flow into the self-aware human I, but only into human physical, etheric, and astral bodies. In other words, a degree of unconsciousness was always necessary for divine spiritual forces to flow into human beings. This state of affairs, however, was meant to change. The Christ was born into the spiritual tradition of the Law of Moses, which addressed only the human astral body. That is, although the law worked in human beings, it did not work directly out of the forces of the I. These forces became possible only in Christ Jesus' time, when individuals first became conscious of the I. Christ Jesus points to this phenomenon in the Luke Gospel when he speaks of John the Baptist as his forerunner (Luke 7:18–35 [cf. Luke 1:16–17 (ed.)]). He says that to receive a completely new principle, people's souls must first become fully mature.

How did the Christ himself view the individuality of John? He saw John as the last to proclaim the best aspects of the past, the purest, noblest form of the teachings of the ancient Prophets. The law and the Prophets culminate in John, whose task was to present his contemporaries with the gifts of old teachings and old soul contents for one final time before the appearance of the Christ. How had these soul contents worked before the Christ principle entered human evolution?

At this point we encounter a phenomenon that the natural sciences would find very strange today but will one day incorporate when they have accepted a bit of inspiration from spiritual science. This subject, which I can touch on only briefly here, will demonstrate how profoundly spiritual science will illuminate the natural sciences. Modern biology, in an attempt to apply the limited faculties of human thinking to explaining the mysteries of human existence, describes how the interaction of male and female germ cells produces a supposedly complete human being. One of the fundamental efforts of modern biology is to prove that an entire human being emerges from this interaction. Cellular substances are examined under the microscope in attempts to determine which characteristics originate in the male gamete and which in the female. However, progress in the field of biology will force it to acknowledge that at our present evolutionary level, only part of the human constitution is determined by the interaction of male and female gametes and that as a rule this interaction does not explain the entire individual, regardless of how exactly we can determine which characteristics come from which gamete.

Each human being contains a virginal element, as it were, which is not stimulated by the fusion of gametes but originates in completely different domains of existence. This element, which unites with a human embryo at conception, does not come from either of the parents, yet it belongs to and is destined for that specific individual. It pours into the I and can be ennobled by receiving the Christ principle, and its birth is virginal. Biological methods will eventually confirm the relationship between this element and the significant transition that occurred at the time of Christ Jesus. Previously, the inner aspect of the individual contained nothing that did not enter via the embryo, but meanwhile changes have occurred in the evolution of the I. Since that time, the human race has changed. A new element has been added to the embryo's makeup, an element that we must now gradually develop and ennoble by receiving the Christ principle.

We are approaching a very subtle truth. For those familiar with modern natural science, it is both strange and interesting to note that already today researchers in certain fields confront the fact that a certain aspect of the human being does not originate in the embryo, but their intellects are not sufficiently advanced to acknowledge the full significance of their experimental observations. Objectively speaking, modern science does not recognize certain elements that influence its experiments. Science would make little progress if it depended exclusively on the skill of laboratory technicians or clinical researchers, but behind them stand the guiding forces of the world, allowing elements to surface that the researchers are instrumental in revealing but do not understand. Even objective research is guided by the "masters," that is, by more advanced individualities, although this state of affairs will remain unrecognized until researchers' conscious faculties become imbued with anthroposophical spiritual teachings.

With the addition of this new element at the time of the Christ's appearance on earth, human faculties underwent a great change. Previously, incarnated human beings had access only to abilities that originated in their paternal and maternal gametes, for only such faculties develop within the human being on the basis of our physical, etheric, and astral bodies. Before the time of Christ Jesus, the tools available to us developed exclusively from the embryo, while afterward a virginal element not stimulated by the embryo was added. If we succumb completely to a merely materialistic perspective, of course this element is degraded, but it can be ennobled and transferred to successive incarnations in an ever more advanced form if we surrender to the warmth emanating from the Christ principle.

What I have just said, however, presupposes that we understand two important points, namely, that all revelations before the time of the Christ were in some way bound to inherited faculties present in the embryo, and that Christ Jesus had to address faculties related to the seed from the divine worlds rather than to the earthly embryo. All the advanced individualities, whether prophets or bodhisattvas, who spoke to human beings before the appearance of Christ Jesus had to use faculties transmitted to them through embryonic potentials. Christ Jesus, however, speaks to the aspect of the human being that does not pass through the embryo but originates in divine realms. That is what he means when he says to his disciples of John the Baptist, "I tell you, among those born of woman none is greater than John, and yet the least in the kingdom of God is greater than he" (Luke 7:28) — that is, John is the greatest of those whose entire being can be explained on the basis of physical birth and male and female gametes, but even the smallest portion of the element that is not "born of woman" but enters the human being from the kingdom of God is greater than John.

Great profundities are concealed in such words. If we allow the essence of spiritual science to illumine our study of the Bible, we will realize that the Bible contains physiological truths that are greater than any discoveries of bungling modern physiology. A verse such as the above is a stimulus to recognizing a great physiological fact. When we truly understand the Bible, profound truths are revealed.

Christ Jesus offers many different examples of the new element he introduced. He pointed out that this element is totally different than all previous revelations because it is proclaimed through faculties that are not inherited but born out of the kingdom of heaven. He indicates how difficult it is for people to gradually rise to a level that allows them to understand the teachings of the Gospel. People want to be persuaded and convinced in the same old ways, but the Christ immediately tells them that the old ways cannot convince them of new truths. A new testimony to the spirit is required, and the sign of the ancient form of initiation, the sign of Jonah, says nothing about the new form. The sign of Jonah symbolized, in the old way, the gradual increase in knowledge that allowed individuals to become initiates or — to use the biblical term — prophets (Luke 11:29–32).

The ancient method of initiation into the spiritual world

involved preparing one's soul to the appropriate level of maturity before spending three and a half days in a state of complete withdrawal from the outer world and the sensory tools used to perceive it. Candidates for initiation were first carefully trained; their souls were prepared to understand the life of the spirit. Then they were taken to a place where for three and a half days their outer senses could perceive nothing and they retreated from the world. A state resembling bodily death was induced in them; their souls were cut off from the outer world and led into a completely different world. After three and a half days they were reawakened, that is, their souls were called back into their bodies. Such people were then able to remember and communicate their perceptions of the higher worlds. All ethnic groups included individuals who were then able to impart information about the spiritual world because they had undergone the experience described in the Bible as Jonah's sojourn in the whale (Jonah 2:1). In ancient times, individuals were carefully prepared for this experience, and when they reappeared to their people, they bore the mark of Jonah to indicate their direct perception of the spiritual world. This was the form of ancient initiation the Christ referred to when he said that the only sign given would be the sign of Jonah (Luke 11:29).

The next verses in the Luke Gospel also describe a second ancient form of initiation. As a legacy of ancient times, some people still became dimly clairvoyant and were guided into the spiritual world through revelation from above, without any effort or activity on their part. Although initiates of this second type lived among ordinary people, their heredity permitted them to receive revelations from above in an enhanced trancelike state without first undergoing a specific initiation process. The Christ pointed out that both types of initiation into the spiritual world had come down from the past. He reminded his listeners about King Solomon as an example of an untrained individual who beheld the spiritual world through revelation from above. Thus the Queen of Sheba, who visited King Solomon, is the bearer of wisdom from above, the representative of all those predestined to possess dim hereditary remnants of the clairvoyance that had been widespread in Atlantean times (Luke 11:31).

Solomon and the symbolic visit of the Queen of Sheba, the queen of the south, represent one type of initiation. The other type, which took place under the sign of Jonah, involved withdrawing totally from the outer world for three and a half days to travel through the spiritual world. After referring to these two types of initiation, the Christ added, "And behold, something greater than Solomon is here" and "Something greater than Jonah is here" (Luke 11:31–32), pointing out a new element of divine revelation that does not simply speak to the human ether body from outside, as in Solomon's case, or from within via a suitably prepared astral body, as in Jonah's case. The new element — the virginal aspect of the human soul — belongs to the kingdom of heaven and unites with the forces of that kingdom when the human I becomes sufficiently mature. Human beings can degrade this aspect by repudiating the Christ principle but can foster and encourage it by imbuing themselves with what emanates from the Christ principle.

The teachings of Christ Jesus, as described in the Luke Gospel, incorporated a new element. As we see, all the old ways of revealing the kingdom of heaven were changed by the event of Palestine. That is why the Christ told those who were at least somewhat prepared to understand him that they would not see the kingdom of heaven simply through revelation, like Solomon, or through initiation under the sign of Jonah; if that was all they achieved, they would die before seeing the kingdom of God in this incarnation. In other words, without being initiated, they would not see the kingdom of God before dying, but in order to be initiated they would have to undergo a deathlike state.

The Christ also meant to show, however, that the new element that had entered the world would now enable some people to see the kingdom of heaven before they died. In a wonderful passage in the Luke Gospel, the Christ speaks of a higher form of revelation: "But I tell you truly, there are some standing here who will not taste death before they see the kingdom of God" (Luke 9:27). Initially, the disciples did not understand the implications of this statement. They did not understand that those standing around the Christ had been chosen to experience the powerful effect of his I, of the Christ principle, which would enable them to ascend directly into the spiritual world. He meant, however, that they themselves would experience the mysteries of the kingdom of heaven before undergoing either natural death or the death of initiation. The spiritual world was to be revealed to them without either the sign of Solomon or the sign of Jonah. Did that indeed happen?

This passage is followed immediately by the scene of Christ's Transfiguration. He led three disciples — Peter, James, and John — up into the spiritual world, where they encountered the spiritual beings not only of Moses and Elijah but also of Christ Jesus himself (Luke 9:28–36). For a moment the disciples beheld the spiritual world and learned that it was possible to do so in a third way, without the sign of Solomon or the sign of Jonah. It was also apparent, however, that they were still beginners, for they were immediately torn out of their physical and etheric bodies by the sheer power of the event. That is why the Christ found them sleeping.

This passage demonstrates a new, third way of entering the spiritual world and tells those who can read the signs of the times that the human I has evolved and can now be directly inspired and influenced by divine forces. At the same time, however, this passage shows that even the most advanced of the Christ's contemporaries were not able to receive the Christ principle completely. Their first actions after the Transfiguration immediately proved their inability. Their forces failed them when they attempted to heal a boy possessed by an evil spirit; they could not do it. The Christ pointed out that they were only in the initial stages of developing this ability and told them that he would have to remain with them for a long time before they would fully acquire it (Luke 9:41). He then healed the boy the disciples could not heal. Pointing again to the great mystery of his incarnation, he said to them, "The Son of man is to be delivered into the hands of men" — that is, the time has come for the ultimate accomplishment of human beings during the earthly phase of evolution to begin to be accessible to all. The time has come for human beings to receive the I and recognize its highest manifestation in the Christ.

"Let these words sink into your ears; for the Son of man is to be delivered into the hands of men." But they did not understand this saying, and it was concealed from them, that they should not perceive it (Luke 9:44-45).

How many people today have understood this passage? Not many, but as time passes more and more people will understand that the I, the Son of man, must be surrendered to human beings.

In the next story in the Luke Gospel, the Christ adds an explanation couched in terms suitable for his contemporaries: "And an argument arose among them as to which of them was the greatest" — that is, who was most suited to receive the Christ principle. "But when Jesus perceived the thought of their hearts, he took a child, and put him by his side, and said to them, "Whoever receives this child in my name receives me, and whoever receives me receives him who sent me" (Luke 9:46–48) — that is, receives the one who sent this part of the human being to earth. The esoteric meaning of this passage emphasizing the importance of fostering the childlike aspect of human nature is that human beings today are the product of ancient forces that worked when Luciferic beings had not yet invaded human beings. The Luciferic forces later concealed themselves in the faculties that modern human beings possess. In everything that originates in the embryo, human consciousness mingles with Luciferic forces that pull human beings down to a lower level. The consciousness human beings developed prior to the Christ's appearance was totally pervaded with Luciferic forces remaining from earlier times. The unconscious, which dates back to evolution on Saturn, Sun, and Moon, when no Luciferic forces were present, is the virginal element, which unites with the human being only when individuals cultivate the Christ principle within themselves. Every human being we encounter today is the result of heredity, of a confluence of elements from parental germ cells, and is thus an intrinsically twofold being. This twofoldness has been pervaded by Luciferic forces. Until individuals are fully illumined by self-awareness, until they can distinguish between good and evil from within the I, their earlier, original nature is visible through the veil of later degradation. Only the childlike element in modern human beings preserves a remnant of human nature as it was before we succumbed to the influence of Luciferic beings.

Thus in the human beings we encounter now, we find a "childlike" part and an "adult" part, as it were, although the adult part, which is pervaded by Luciferic forces, asserts itself from the very beginning of embryonic development. Because even children are already imbued with Luciferic forces, the pre-Luciferic element is not evident in ordinary life. It must be resurrected by the power of the Christ, which unites with the best forces of our original, childlike nature. This power cannot unite with degraded faculties, with the products of merely intellectual knowledge. It must unite with the best aspect of human nature, with the childlike remnant that persists from ancient times. It regenerates this remnant first, as a starting-point for revivifying the rest of the human being.

As modern human beings, we may possess excellent potentials; we may develop these potentials and make good progress on the level of ordinary life. We typically do not consider the unconscious, however, and it is important to consider this childlike element because it provides an initial point of entry for the Christ faculty, which reenlivens all our other faculties. We must begin by making this childlike element wise and then move on to make our other faculties wise again. In this respect, each of us carries a childlike nature within us which, when it becomes active, is receptive to uniting with the Christ principle. In contrast, if only Luciferic forces are at work in us (no matter how exalted they may be), they will deny and mock the Christ force that manifests in earthly life, as the Christ himself predicted.

The Luke Gospel clearly presents the meaning of the new revelation. In ancient times, only those who had been taught to recognize the mark of Jonah knew that the initiates who bore that sign could convey information about the spiritual world. Specific preparation was required to recognize the mark of Jonah or the mark of Solomon. Now a new preparation is needed to produce a new type of understanding and a new way of maturing the soul. Initially, the contemporaries of Christ Jesus were only able to understand the old, familiar way presented by John the Baptist. People were alienated by Christ Jesus' completely new way and by his selection of souls who did not look like traditional candidates for initiation. People assumed that Christ Jesus would preach to those involved in traditional practices and could not understand why he sat with people whom they considered sinners. But he said: If I used old forms to present the new element I am bringing to humankind instead of replacing the old forms with new ones, that would be like patching an old cloak with a piece of new cloth or putting new wine in old wineskins. Humankind must receive this new element, which is more than the marks of Solomon or Jonah, in new wineskins and new forms. You must brace yourselves to receive the new proclamation (Luke 5:36–37).

Traditional learning did not allow Christ Jesus' contemporaries to understand this message. It can be understood only through the mighty influence of the I, through the element that flowed into human beings from the spiritual being of the Christ. Those destined to receive this element were not the students of old, traditional teachings but those who had undergone incarnation after incarnation yet remained simple people who understood through the power of faith that flowed into them. These people also had to be given a sign, a sign for all eyes to see. The "mystic death" initiates had undergone for millennia in the mystery temples had to be replayed on the great stage of world history. The mysteries emerged from the great initiation temples and were played out in a single event on Golgotha, a mighty, public representation of what initiates alone once witnessed during the three and a half days of ancient initiation rites. Knowledgeable people recognized the event of Golgotha as an initiation transferred to the stage of world history. Formerly, candidates for initiation spent three and a half days in a state of deathlike repose that convinced them that the spirit will always overcome bodily nature and that the human soul and spirit belong to a spiritual world. This process, formerly witnessed only by the few, by initiates in the mystery temples, was now played out in public for all the world to see. The event of Golgotha was an initiation rite performed not in an intimate setting for a few close witnesses but on the stage of world history, for all of humankind to see.

From the drops of blood that fell from Christ Jesus' wounds as he hung on the cross on Golgotha, a stream of spiritual life flows into all human beings. The wisdom that once flowed from other messengers of the spiritual world now flows into humankind as a living force. This is the great difference between the event of Golgotha and the teachings of other religions.

Correctly interpreting what happened on Golgotha requires a more profound understanding than exists today. At the beginning of the Earth phase of evolution, the human I was linked to the physical substance of the blood. Blood is the outer expression of the human I. If the Christ had not appeared, human beings would have continued to strengthen the I and would have devolved into egotism. This was prevented by the event of Golgotha. Blood, the excess substance of the I, had to be shed. This process began when the sweat fell from the Redeemer's brow like drops of blood on the Mount of Olives and continued when the blood flowed from his wounds on Golgotha. This blood was a sign of the need to sacrifice excess egotism in human nature. That is why we must investigate the spiritual significance of the Christ's sacrifice on Golgotha on a more profound level. The truth of what happened on Golgotha is not apparent to chemistry or to a superficial intellectual view. Chemical analysis of the blood that flowed on Golgotha would reveal the same substances that other human blood contains, but esoteric methods reveal that this blood is different. It is the excess that would have led human beings into egotism if infinite love had not appeared and allowed this blood to flow. Esoteric research reveals that infinite love mingles with this blood, completely pervading it.

Each Evangelist has a particular role and a particular emphasis, and the author of the Luke Gospel was especially concerned with depicting the infinite love that flowed into the world through the Christ and will gradually drive out egotism. If we could illuminate the esoteric connections among the Gospels on a more profound level, we would find that these connections resolve all the seeming contradictions discovered by materialistic research, just as the contradictions in the Gospel accounts of the early years of Jesus of Nazareth are resolved when we learn the facts of his childhood. Each of the Evangelists described what was most obvious to his own perspective. Hence, Luke describes what his sources — "independent seers" and "servants of the word" — were specially trained to perceive. The other Evangelists perceived other aspects of the life of Christ Jesus, but the author of the Luke Gospel perceived the outpouring of love that forgives even the most terrible offense in the physical world. The words that resound from the cross on Golgotha express this ideal love: "Father, forgive them, for they know not what they do" (Luke 23:34). This infinite love that forgives even the ultimate offense becomes a reality when Christ Jesus, hanging on the cross on Golgotha, begs forgiveness for his crucifiers.

The Luke Gospel is also the gospel of the power of faith. It emphasizes that human nature includes an outpouring element whose purpose is to extricate individuals from the sensory world, regardless of how deeply they are entwined in it. Imagine individuals who have grown one with the sensory world through all sorts of crimes and have been punished by the courts of the physical world. Let's imagine that one such individual has preserved the germ of the power of faith, while another has not. This is the difference between the two criminals crucified with Christ Jesus. One had no faith, and his sentence was executed. The other, however, retained a faint glimmer of faith that illumined the spiritual world so that he could not lose his connection to it. This is why the Christ says to him, "Truly, I say to you, today" — since you recognize your connection to the spiritual world — "you will be with me in Paradise" (Luke 23:34). In the Luke Gospel, therefore, the truths that resound from the cross include faith and hope as well as love.

One thing remains to be achieved in the soul domain emphasized by the author of the Luke Gospel. Imbued with the love that streams down from the cross on Golgotha, we can see into the future. We realize that as the Earth phase of

evolution progresses, the spirit in human beings must gradually transform all of physical, earthly existence. The father
principle that we received before the Luciferic influence began will gradually recede, but we will allow our whole spirit to
be pervaded by the Christ principle, and our hands will express clear images that live in our souls. Our hands were created not by us but by the father principle, and in the future
they will be imbued with the Christ principle. As we pass from
incarnation to incarnation, our accomplishments in the physical body will incorporate the spiritual element that flows from
the mystery of Golgotha into the father principle, that is, the
Christ principle that pervades the outer world. We will emulate the composure streaming down from the cross on
Golgotha, which becomes the highest hope and ideal for the
future: I allow faith and love to sprout within me. They will
live and grow in me; when they grow strong enough, they will
pervade my entire physical aspect, the father principle within
me. Hope for our human future will be added to faith and
love, and human beings will acquire the composure needed to
face the future: If I have faith and love, I may hope that the
Christ in me will gradually flow outward. Then human beings
will understand the great ideal of the words that resounded
from the cross, "Father, into thy hands I commit my spirit"
(Luke 23:46).

Words of love, faith, and hope resound from the cross in
the Gospel that describes the confluence of previously separate spiritual currents in the soul of Jesus of Nazareth. The
great Christ ideal streamed into mere knowledge and transformed it into a soul force. The human soul's task is to gain an
ever better understanding of what the Luke Gospel reveals, an
understanding that will increasingly enliven the three ideals

resounding from the cross. The faculties that spiritual scientific truths foster in us allow us to experience the words resounding from the cross as a living proclamation rather than as mere dead words. We begin to understand that religious documents such as the Luke Gospel conceal a living word that spiritual science must gradually reveal.

In this lecture cycle, we attempted to fathom as much as possible of the profound meaning of the Luke Gospel. Of course a single lecture series cannot reveal all aspects of a document with such universal content, and much must remain unexplained. If you follow the path outlined in this cycle, however, you will discover ever more profound truths, and your souls will become increasingly receptive to the living word concealed behind the outer words. Spiritual science, or theosophy, is not a new doctrine. It is a tool for understanding what humankind is given at any point in time. At the moment, spiritual science is a tool for understanding the religious documents of Christian revelation. If you see anthroposophical spiritual science in this light, you will no longer call it Christian theosophy or a different form of theosophy. There is only one theosophy, one spiritual science, one single tool for revealing the truth. We use this tool to unearth the treasures of humankind's spiritual life. Spiritual science is the tool for unearthing the treasures of the Bhagavad Gita in one instance and of the Luke Gospel in another. The greatness of the spiritual scientific movement lies in its ability to plumb to the depths any of the spirit's gifts to humankind, and we would misunderstand it if we closed our minds to any of the various revelations that have been proclaimed to human beings throughout the ages.

I hope you will receive the proclamation of the Luke Gos-

pel in this sense and understand how completely it is pervaded
by the inspiration of love. If you do, the insight into this Gospel that spiritual science provides will continue to grow in your
souls and will help to illumine not only the mysteries of the
periphery — that is, the spiritual foundations of existence —
but also the meaning of those very fundamental words, "peace
in human hearts in whom goodwill dwells." More than any
other document, the Luke Gospel, if fully understood, fills
human souls with the warm love that allows peace to dwell on
earth as the most exquisite reflection of divine mysteries. Revelations must be reflected on earth, reflected back into the
spiritual heights. If we acknowledge spiritual science in this
sense, it will reveal the mysteries of divine spiritual beings and
spiritual existence, and the reflection of these revelations will
dwell in our souls as love and peace, the most exquisite earthly
reflection of what streams down to us from the heights.

This is the true significance of the words that resound in
the Luke Gospel when the strength of the Buddha's *nirmanakaya* pours into the Nathanic infant Jesus. Revelations from
spiritual worlds stream down to earth and are reflected in
human hearts as love and peace inasmuch as human beings
evolve toward the goodwill that the Christ principle causes to
unfold and flow from the human core, the I. When we understand the Luke Gospel correctly, this message resounds both
clearly and warmly from the words, "Spiritual worlds are revealed from the heights and reflected back by human hearts,
bringing peace to human beings on earth who freely choose
to develop true goodwill in the course of the Earth phase of
evolution."

NOTES

1. See Rudolf Steiner, *The Gospel of St. John and Its Relation to the Other Gospels*. Spring Valley, N.Y.: Anthroposophic Press, 1982 (GA 112, *Das Johannes-Evangelium im Verhältnis zu den drei anderen Evangelien, besonders zu dem Lukas-Evangelium*).

2. Emil Bock identifies this "later individuality" as the founder of Manichean Christianity and says that Rudolf Steiner himself makes this association. Cf. Emil Bock, *The Three Years*. London: Christian Community Press, 1969. —*Trans.*

Rudolf Steiner's Ten Lectures on the Gospel of Luke: A Descriptive Outline

ROBERT A. McDERMOTT

Lecture One:
The Four Gospels in the Light of Anthroposophy

IN THE FIRST OF THESE LECTURES, Rudolf Steiner revealed
to his audience in Basel, Switzerland, the fruits of his spiritual-scientific research concerning the thoughts and visions
that enabled Luke to write his Gospel. In this lecture, Steiner
offers a brief characterization of the four evangelists and their
Gospels, each of which he develops in a full cycle of lectures.
Just prior to these lectures, Rudolf Steiner had published *An
Outline of Esoteric Science*, his major work on the evolution of
the earth and humanity and on the process of initiation, and
lecture cycles on the Gospel of John, the Apocalypse of John

and on the Gospel of John in relation to the other Gospels. In the year to follow, he delivered lecture cycles on the background to the Gospel of Mark and on the Gospel of Matthew. In each of these cycles, Steiner offers comparisons and contrasts of the Gospel writers and their texts: he invariably refers to John as the most profound, but he also emphasizes that Luke offers a sensitivity and healing power unlike anything available in John.

In brief, Steiner says we should turn to the Gospel of John for brilliant and powerful intuitions and for the experience of union with a divine being, such as John reveals in relation to the Logos. The Gospel of John is ideal for the mystical soul, while Luke's is ideal for the humble soul. Luke offers imaginations, such as pictures of the Nativity, as well as colors, lights, and sounds of spiritual beings. Matthew and Luke excel at imaginative cognition, particularly the pictures of the lineage of Jesus as revealed in the Akashic record. Steiner also explains the difficulties involved in tracking individuals who lived in the historical past because each human life is composed of four parts — the physical body, the etheric (or life) body, the astral (or soul) body, and the ego (or "I").

Steiner explained three higher ways of knowing in his foundational books, especially his *Outline of Esoteric Science*, published the same year as *According to Luke*. *Imagination* refers to the observation of an inner transformation such as of a plant in process of growth followed by its decay. *Inspiration* refers to the observation of a process such as growth and decay as such, independent of an object like a plant. Whereas imagination refers to the inner process of a changing image, and inspiration refers to the observation of one's own soul process, *intuition* is independent of both images and one's soul process, and refers instead to a state of consciousness of the spiritual world independent of both outer and inner stimulation.

These three higher ways of knowing correspond to higher realities just as the usual way of knowing — sensory experience assimilated by intellect — is adequate only to sense-perceptible realities and is consequently inadequate for understanding the realities depicted in the four Gospels. This emphasis on levels of knowledge is well-established in Hindu and Buddhist traditions, as it was in medieval Christian philosophy and theology, but is often neglected in modern Western thinking, including thinking about the Gospels. Throughout his writings and lectures, Steiner emphasizes this need for *adaequatio* — utilizing a level of thinking adequate to the level of reality to be known.

The conflicting accounts of the Nativity of Jesus in the Gospels of Matthew and Luke call for a very high degree of cognitive adequacy: the pictures to be reconciled, or newly understood, require a level and purity of imagination adequate to the two stories which have been merged in Christian art and piety but which, in terms of the accounts themselves, are difficult to reconcile. At the outset of these ten lectures, Steiner calls on a level of imagination that most readers will find daunting. Yet the pictures he presents might eventually gain plausibility, particularly when supplemented by his accounts of the contributions by higher beings such as Hermes, Moses, Zoroaster, and Buddha.

At the conclusion of the first lecture, Steiner briefly lists the contrasts and apparent contradictions between the Nativity narratives of Matthew and Luke. Here, in summary form, are the differences to which Steiner repeatedly returns in this lecture cycle and claims to reconcile by asserting that both versions are true, and part of a much larger, deeper, and more mysterious narrative (a more complete summary of which can be found in the descriptive outline of Lecture Four, pp. 237-38):

> **Matthew:** The birth of Jesus is announced beforehand to Joseph (1:20). The Magi come from the East (2:2); the ire of Herod, and the escape of Mary, Joseph, and Jesus into Egypt (2:13). They return not to Bethlehem but to Nazareth (2:23).

> **Luke:** The annunciation was made to Mary (1:28). The newborn Jesus is visited not by Magi but by shepherds (2:17). There is no mention of a flight to Egypt; Joseph and Mary found the twelve-year-old Jesus teaching the rabbis in the temple.

Lecture Two:
Buddha and the Gospel of Luke

In this lecture Rudolf Steiner introduces the beautiful, if astonishing, idea that Buddha was involved in the birth of Jesus. Steiner also indicates that Luke the healer and teacher of forgiveness would be the ideal evangelist to see and paint in words this picture of Buddha in collaboration with Christ. Immediately following the annunciation of the birth of Jesus to shepherds watching their flocks by night, Luke presents one of the most celebrated announcements in the New Testament: "And suddenly there was with the angel a heavenly host, praising God and saying, 'Glory to God in the heaven, and on earth peace among those whom he favors'" (2:14).

Steiner's spiritual-scientific research led him to report that this angelic choir was in fact the glorified Buddha:

The image that appeared to the shepherds was the transfigured Buddha, the spiritual figure of the bodhisattva of ancient times, the being who had brought the message of love and compassion to human beings for millennia. Now that this being had completed his final earthly incarnation, he hovered in spiritual heights and appeared to the shepherds beside the angel who proclaimed what was to happen in Palestine.

These are the findings of spiritual investigation. It was the bodhisattva of old who now, in the glory of Buddhahood, appeared to the shepherds (p. 55).

A reader not familiar with Steiner's esoteric research might well ask (or exclaim), how did Buddha get into the Nativity of Jesus? The concept of the Mahayana, amply understood, goes a long way toward providing a framework for an answer to this question, and to claims concerning the unexpected role of higher beings, including the role of Buddha and other spiritual figures, in the development of Jesus of Nazareth. In contrast to early Buddhist schools, which they called Hinayana (the "narrow" or "lesser vehicle"), the later Buddhist schools called themselves Mahayana (the "greater vehicle"). The Mahayana tradition explains the reality of Buddha by the concept of the bodhisattva.

For the Hinayana tradition, the only surviving school of which is called Theravada (or the "way of the elders"), Gautama Buddha attained enlightenment and taught others to do likewise. After his enlightenment experience, Buddha ("he who awoke") taught his disciples to be lights unto themselves. The Mahayana tradition, however, regards Buddha as an infinite and eternal being who incarnates as a bodhisattva who works for humanity until such time as humanity can receive his message. The bodhisattva born in northeast India in the sixth century B.C. incarnated in order to teach compassion and love, and was able to have these qualities become permanent human capacities. It was precisely these lofty human qualities, first incarnated through Buddha in the sixth century B.C., that the shepherds saw on display above the infant Jesus and his parents, and that rayed into the infant for the further evolution of all humanity.

Steiner's research concerning the events in the life of Jesus of Nazareth reveal a thoroughly Mahayanist perspective: Buddha, the bodhisattvas, Hermes, Moses, Zoroaster, and Krishna are beings who have contributed particular capacities to various levels of the human being, including the etheric or life-principle, soul, and spirit. According to Steiner, six centuries after he made the transition from bodhisattva to Buddha, Buddha rayed his infinite love and compassion into the infant Jesus. It was this inspiring contribution that the shepherds were allowed to witness in the stable in Bethlehem.

This transmission included not only Buddha's teaching concerning love and compassion, but equally his enlightenment, made possible by his overcoming the brute fact of suffering or *dukkha*. The facts of Buddha's enlightenment — his experience of the three sorrows and the monks, his temptation by Mara, his holding to the middle way between asceticism and indulgence, his conclusion that suffering arises in desire and can be cured by the eightfold path — are increasingly well-known at the present time, but were completely unknown to Theophilus and the community of Gentile Christians of the late first century for whom Luke was writing his Gospel.

In this lecture, Steiner includes three teachings, or disciplines, that Gautama follows as preparation for the realization of Buddhahood or enlightenment. Gautama absorbed important components of the Samkhya philosophy, one of the six so-called orthodox philosophical systems in the Indian tradition. Samkhya developed during the century before the birth of Buddha and was formulated systematically in the *Shamkyakarika* ("Treatise on Shamkhya"), by Ishvarakrṣna (an Indian philosopher named after Lord Krishna, the author of the Bhagavad Gita). The *Shamkyakarika* opens with a statement that clearly shows the similarity of Samkhya to the experience and teaching of Buddha concerning suffering: "From the torment of pain there arises the desire to know how to stop all pain."

In a way similar to the teachings of Zoroaster in Persia at approximately the same century as Buddha, Samkhya posits an ultimate metaphysical dualism: *puruṣa* (spirit) and *prakṛti* (matter). *Puruṣa* neither produces nor is produced; it does, however, "'entice' *prakṛti* into activity by 'dancing before it,' with the result that *prakṛti* is induced to go from an unmanifest state of pure potentiality into manifestation, pure activity or evolution. As a result the worlds are brought forth."[1]

According to the *Shamkyakarika*, and the Samkhya teaching available to Gautama, *puruṣa* sees *prakṛti*, as a result of which *prakṛti* ceases all activity (and thereby all suffering); *puruṣa*, once liberated, continues in existence even though it does not need to. It is a short step from this teaching to Buddha's doctrine of enlightenment: there is no self, but it is perfectly fine to continue in existence in such a way that the delusion of self (*prakṛti*) no longer causes the delusory self to suffer.

After Gautama experienced the four passing sights, he announced to his father and his wife that he would leave them in order to go to the forest to find the solution to the problem of *dukkha* (suffering, impermanence). During the next seven years, until he achieved enlightenment (the cessation of suffering), Gautama practiced the eight steps of the classical yoga system that Patanjali, in his *Yoga Sutras*, had systematically rendered at the same time as Buddha. This text, famous in the West as well as in Asian cultures, teaches eight steps or "limbs": the first two concern moral preparation, the next three concern the external or physical, and the last three concern the internal:

- *Yama*: five abstentions
- *Niyama*: five observances
- *Āsana*: balanced posture
- *Prāṇayāma*: regularity of breath
- *Pratayara*: withdrawal of the senses
- *Dhāranā*: concentration
- *Dhyāṇa*: meditation
- *Samādhi*: contemplation

Buddha did not teach these steps as such but since he practiced them on his way to enlightenment, the dharma (as path, and distinct from his dharma as doctrine) that he taught includes them implicitly. Buddha taught moral preparation, concentration of breathing and the senses, and then several levels of meditation. Similar to Patanjali's *Yoga Sutras*, the Buddha's emphasis is on the path, or the practice, rather than on any particular doctrine — except for the doctrine of no-self, which Buddha considered essential as an aid to the overcoming of desire (and thereby *dukkha*).

Buddha also learned from various ascetics. A favorite artistic image in the Buddhist tradition is Gautama before his enlightenment, sitting in a yogic position and emaciated as a result of extreme fasting. While this practice no doubt helped him develop whatever additional determination and control he might have needed on his way, once he attained enlightenment he eschewed asceticism in favor of the middle way: neither by fasting nor by indulgence can the way to enlightenment be attained.

Steiner traces the Buddha's evolution, describing how he worked as a bodhisattva and how he realized his potentiality as Buddha. Before he attained Buddhahood, Gautama of course relied on scriptural texts, teachers and exemplars, particularly the teaching of Samkhya philosophy and the yoga practices of various ascetics. Because he was already a bodhisattva and an initiate, he was not as dependent on these teachings and teachers as others have been, and he was able to discover for himself what he needed to realize and to teach. This account combines elements from both the Theravada tradition, which focuses on Gautama (the human dimension of Buddha), and the Mahayana, which focuses on the transcendent and universal, immanent dimension of Buddha. In the West, the most famous Theravada account of Buddha is the novel *Siddhartha* by Hermann Hesse, in which Siddhartha, who is striving to attain enlightenment, meets the historical Buddha, but turns away from the opportunity to become a disciple in order to follow his own path. Hesse makes it clear that the main character of his book was right to resist discipleship.

In Steiner's account, some of this independence is also prized, as it is in the path of initiation he taught in the foundational books he wrote just a few years before the lecture cycle on the Gospel of Luke: *How to Know Higher Worlds* (1904), *Theosophy* (1904), and *An Outline of Esoteric Science* (1909).

Unlike Hesse and other exponents of the Theravada view, Steiner also emphasizes that Gautama became the Buddha because he had already been a bodhisattva and reincarnated in order to bring to humanity what he would achieve and would be prepared to exemplify and teach in that life. By virtue of his own karma (created by previous lives, which were characterized by great spiritual achievements), and with the help of the spiritual world, the bodhisattva who became Buddha in the sixth century B.C. reincarnated ever so close to Buddhahood. When he experienced "the four sights" — the three sorrows (illness, old age and death), followed by the line of monks in walking meditation — Gautama the bodhisattva knew what he had to do to realize his destiny as Buddha.

Lecture 3:
Buddha's Contribution to Humanity

In this third lecture Steiner continues describing the contribution of Buddha to the infant Jesus, and through him to the whole of humanity. Once again Steiner describes Buddha as a great initiate who brought one of the greatest of all teachings to humanity. He also indicates that as a teacher and exemplar of balance, Buddha inevitably struggled against the two tempters, Lucifer and Ahriman, both fabulously adept at unbalancing humanity. Buddha understood that because of the negative, or unbalancing, influence of Lucifer (who convinces humanity that it is more enlightened than it is) and Ahriman (who convinces humanity that it should go deeper into matter at the expense of the spiritual), humanity suffers from a craving for existence. It is the suffering (*dukkha*) due to this craving that Buddha sought to cure by his teaching and the power of his compassion during the lifetime when he served humanity

directly on earth, and subsequently in collaboration with Jesus
Christ.

Ever since his first sermon, immediately following his enlightenment experience, Buddha and Buddhism have been
identified with the Four Noble Truths and with the doctrine
of no-self. In his first sermon, delivered to his fellow seekers
(who had been disappointed in him because he had given up
the practice of asceticism), Buddha taught truths which are
simple to state but difficult to fathom completely or to practice perfectly:

- All existence is characterized by *dukkha* (suffering,
  pain, impermanence, incompleteness, dissatisfaction);
- *Dukkha* is caused by desire (by a thirst for existence
  centered in the self even though, or because, the self
  as such is illusory);
- It is possible for human beings to eliminate in their
  own lives the cause of *dukkha* (and therefore of
  suffering);
- The process of overcoming *dukkha* is the eightfold
  path:
  > Right view
  > Right judgment
  > Right speech
  > Right action
  > Right vocation
  > Right habit
  > Right mindfulness
  > Right contemplation

Based on his own direct spiritual-scientific experience of
Buddha, Steiner uses the Mahayanist concept of *trikaya*, or

"three bodies," to explain the complex reality of Buddha. These three terms are generally understood in Buddhist schools as follows:

Dharmakaya: literally, "truth body"; Buddha's infinite and eternal body. This body causes the other two bodies so as to let them appear to be real, even though they are ultimately identical with Dharmakaya.

Sambhogakaya: literally, "bliss body"; Gautama's spiritual body. This body includes the bodhisattvas, and focuses more on the bodhisattva realm than on the historical Buddha.

Nirmanakaya: literally, "assumed body," "manifest body"; Buddha's incarnational body, the body of Gautama. This body proceeds from Dharmakaya and despite appearances is really one with Dharmakaya.

In these lectures, Steiner uses the term Nirmanakaya to refer to Buddha in his nonphysical body (presumably etheric and astral). In this respect, it would seem that he should have used the term Sambhogakaya. Since Steiner's references to Buddha in these lectures are very specifically to the Buddha of the sixth century B.C., he might have understood the terms correctly and chosen Nirmanakaya to give this historical emphasis. It should nevertheless be acknowledged that a Buddhist reading this text would find the application of Nirmanakaya (ordinarily the physical incarnation of Buddha) for a spiritual appearance of Buddha (for example, as a choir at the Nativity) at least confusing and probably incorrect.

Steiner says it was the Nirmanakaya Buddha that revealed itself to the shepherds so that they would attend the Nativity

of Jesus. At the event in the Temple, when the twelve-year-old
Jesus (as described in the Luke Gospel) was teaching the
learned rabbis, the astral sheath (covering) of the Jesus described in Matthew united with, and so vitalized, the
Nirmanakaya Buddha (or, perhaps more correctly, Sambhogakaya) that when it entered the Luke-Jesus he was able to
speak with a power which would previously have been
impossible.

Lecture Four:
Formation of the Nathan-Jesus Child

Rudolf Steiner definitely did not adhere to the advice of the
Roman poet Horace, who, in his *Ars Poetica*, cautions writers
not to begin every poem or story "with the twin eggs," that is,
with the founding of Rome by the twins Remus and Romulus.
It is characteristic of Steiner's spiritual-scientific research and
of his account of important events in history to begin at the
beginning, or as close to the beginning as practical. In this case
he follows form by placing the Jesus child described in Luke
within the context of the evolution of consciousness, beginning with the earliest groups of human beings, long prior to
Adam and Eve.

According to the evolution of consciousness which Steiner
had researched through the entire first quarter of the twentieth century, and which he had recounted first in his cycle of
lectures published as *Cosmic Memory* (1904) and *An Outline
of Esoteric Science*, the Adam and Eve event in Genesis is mythi-
cally and in any case archetypally essentially true but omits
important events that prepared the way for it. Steiner's description of the early development of humanity includes the
contributions of spiritual beings of warmth and will, and the

slow development of the human being, including, in succession, the physical body, the etheric body, the astral and the Ego (Spirit, "I").

Steiner indicates that the Adam and Eve event occurred during Lemuria, the 15,000-year period prior to the evolution and destruction of Atlantis. Steiner reports that Atlantis was a 15,000-year period before the post-Atlantean, the 15,000-year period in which we are now living. Steiner says the post-Atlantean period will have seven epochs, of which the current one, the fifth, began in the fifteenth century and is expected to last until the thirty-sixth century. (Steiner's expectations with respect to the future are not to be taken as necessary or determined.)

The Luke-Nathan Jesus was a completely pure soul, not having experienced the Fall in the Garden of Eden. This soul made three sacrifices for humanity prior to incarnating as the Luke-Jesus. In a very real sense, this soul, which was a part of Adam that had not experienced the Fall, is rightly referred to as the Second Adam. But this soul, not having had a previous earthly life, was quite simple, and, as indicated in the next several lectures, was in need of the wisdom and concern for the external world which it received from Zarathustra.

Steiner considered Manu, the teacher of the seven holy *rishis* (or sages) at the beginning of the post-Atlantean period, to be in effect the founder of civilization. Following directly from Manu's teaching, seven epochs are expected to unfold, the first of which was an ancient Indian civilization. This civilization, which predates historical record, was the seed-form of the Indian civilization known through the remains of Mohenja Daro and through the ancient Indian Vedic and Upanishadic texts. The second epoch was the Persian, founded by Zarathustra (literally "golden" or "splendid star"), teacher of the dualism of good and evil. Steiner also attributes to Zarathustra the gift of agriculture.

There is, however, no certain historical knowledge concerning Zarathustra. Even the century in which he might have lived is disputed, with many scholars assigning him to the fifth or sixth century B.C. (making him a contemporary of Buddha, Second Isaiah, Jeremiah, and the Presocratic philosophers), while others place him perhaps five or six centuries earlier. Steiner places Zarathustra in the seventh or eighth *millennium* B.C., but also indicates that in the sixth century B.C., at the same century as some scholars locate Zarathustra, the being who had already lived as Zarathustra reincarnated in Chaldea as Zarathas (or Nazarathos). Steiner indicates in this lecture that this individual was the teacher of the Greek mathematician Pythagoras.

According to Steiner, the original Zarathustra (of the seventh or eighth millennium B.C.) brought to humanity the gift of looking outward as well as efficiency and effectiveness in the world. This influence will have taken hold by the time of Buddha, in the sixth century B.C. — perhaps six or seven millennia later — as a result of which Buddha needed to teach a greater awareness of the inner life. By the time of Jesus, particularly in the part of the world dominated by Roman practicality, there was an intense need for the kind of inner awareness which he taught and exemplified.

The extent of Zarathustra's influence continued through his gifts to individualities who were essential for the development of Egyptian and Hebraic culture. Steiner states that Zarathustra bequeathed his astral (soul) body to Hermes, the esoteric teacher of ancient Egypt, while to Moses he transmitted his etheric (life principle) body. Most remarkably, Zarathustra gave his own ego (or "I") to the formation of the Jesus of Nazareth described in the Matthew Gospel. In the usual account of the Nativity of Jesus in the Christian tradition, the babe in the manger is believed to be the Christ. Steiner's research leads him to an account which is no less dramatic but in a quite unexpected way — as summarized below. As will become clear in the seventh lecture, Steiner reports that Christ incarnated in a human being not at birth but at age thirty when he was baptized in the Jordan River by his cousin John.

Given the story that Steiner tells in this and several subsequent lecture cycles, it is apt that he reminds the reader that if the workings of a machine requires complex explanations, as well as a strenuous effort to understand, surely profound spiritual realities, events that have decisively affected the entire course of human development, should not be expected to be as simple as we wish and expect. The events about to be described are indeed sublime, and not simple. Steiner here reveals that according to his clairvoyant research, the Jesus child described by Luke, born in a stable of poor parents and visited by the shepherds, is not the same child as that described by Matthew, born in a house to middle-aged and middle-class parents, visited by the Magi. Steiner teaches that there were two children named Jesus, each with parents named Joseph and Mary. The two families lived near each other in Nazareth in a friendly relationship. Steiner does not indicate what they understood about their destinies as individuals, as families, and in their collective karmic roles on behalf of the redemption of humanity.

The account that Steiner presents in the last three pages of this lecture needs to be read several times, and probably absorbed with the help of careful notes. There are surely many ways to organize this complex, and quite startling, material, one of which would be as follows:

Scripture source	Gospel of Matthew	Gospel of Luke
Historical lineage	From Abraham, David, and Solomon (1:1–17)	Adam, Abraham, David, and Nathan (3:23–38)
Parents	Middle-aged; of royal lineage; first live in Bethlehem, then Nazareth.	Young and poor; live in Nazareth.
Birth	Several months after the Luke child; in a comfortable setting.	In a stable in Bethlehem, where Joseph and Mary register for the census (2:1–7).
Visitation	Magi from the East (2:1–12)	Shepherds (2:8–20)
Soul/spiritual entity	Zarathustra-"I"	Soul of Buddha and soul of Adam
Characteristics	Wise and kingly	Pure and loving

Scripture source	Gospel of Matthew	Gospel of Luke
Annunciation	To Joseph (1:20)	To Mary (1:28)
Threat by Herod	Family flees to Egypt; later settles in Nazareth near the Luke family (2:13–23).	Threat not mentioned; Jesus remains in Nazareth (2:51–53) until his baptism at age 30.
Teaching in the Temple	The Zarathustra-"I" leaves this Jesus and unites with the Buddha soul of the Luke Jesus.	Luke Jesus acquires kingly bearing from Matthew Jesus; begins to teach learned rabbis (2:41–49).
Two families	Matthew child dies soon after the age of 12. Joseph also dies. The mother of the Matthew child marries the Joseph who is the father of the Luke child and who brings several children who become Jesus's stepbrothers and sisters.	Mary dies. Joseph marries the mother of the now-deceased Matthew child. Jesus's stepmother is spiritually bound to the Christ of the Luke child throughout his later life and in Christian devotion.

Lecture 5:
Contributions to the Nathan Jesus from Buddha and Zarathustra

One of the remarkable components of Steiner's lectures on the Gospel of Luke is its disclosures concerning the importance of Zarathustra in relation to the Incarnation and mission of Christ. Steiner's account of Zarathustra throughout these pages gives the reader a great opportunity for mystery and meditation. The name Zarathustra is known to the modern West in relation to the almost extinct religious teaching that bears his name and as the prophetic messenger of the teaching of the Superman (*Uebermensch*) in Nietzsche's hyperdramatic masterpiece, *Thus Spake Zarathustra* (1891). It is surprising, then, that Zoroaster, the obscure Persian prophet of the dualism of dark and light and the voice of Nietzsche's apocalyptic philosophy, should appear in this lecture cycle as the major contributor, with Buddha, not only to the creation of Jesus of Nazareth but also to the evolution of humanity.

In *Thus Spake Zarathustra*, the prophet of the Superman (or Overman) is the passionate spokesman for the Dionysian (the frenzied and untrammeled will), in contrast to the Apollonian (representing order and reason). But Steiner, both in this cycle and in a lecture on Zarathustra a year and a half later (January 11, 1911), identifies Zarathustra with Apollo, the Greek archetypal expression of order. In so doing, Steiner contrasts Zarathustra not with the Dionysian but with the mystical element characteristic of the Indian stream from the Vedas to Buddha. Steiner also attributes to Zarathustra, again in contrast to the Indian stream, a teaching that emphasizes the external world, especially the cosmological. This contribution is evident in the figures of world significance whom he influenced directly — Hermes, Moses, Pythagoras, Matthew (Solomonic) Jesus, and Luke (Nathanic) Jesus.

Zarathustra gave his astral body to Hermes in order that Zarathustra's vast knowledge of the outer world could be communicated to humanity through the Egyptian esoteric tradition. Zarathustra gave his etheric body to Moses so as to enable Moses to transmit to the Hebrews, and thereby to the ancient Mediterranean world, the pictures of creation presented in Genesis. Through his incarnation as Zarathos or Nazarathos, Zarathustra was "the teacher of Pythagoras and again acquired profound insight into the phenomenal world." Zarathustra did not directly influence Buddha, but according to Steiner, Zarathustra and Buddha represented the two major spiritual streams prior to Christ — Buddha the teacher of the inner life, and Zarathustra the teacher of the external world.

It was the individuality, the ego or spirit, of Zarathustra who incarnated as the Jesus child described in Matthew and who was visited by the three Magi, who were students of Zarathustra. The Magi saw in the "Star of Splendor" the being of Zarathustra, and followed his star to the Nativity in Bethlehem, bringing with them three gifts, symbols of worldly knowledge. The Luke (Nathanic) Jesus, at age twelve, was able to lecture the rabbis in the Temple because the Zarathustra ego had entered him, having just left the Matthew (Solomonic) Jesus. The Jesus previously inhabited by Zarathustra died soon after. Once infused by the Zarathustra ego, the Luke Jesus immediately acquired wisdom to the astonishment of all who had known him, including his parents.

As Steiner explains at the end of the third lecture, Zarathustra awakened by wisdom the compassion of the pure Buddha soul of the Luke Jesus. The Jesus who returned to

Nazareth spent the next eighteen years interweaving the wisdom of Zarathustra with the compassion of Buddha. This joining of Zarathustra and Buddha in the soul of Jesus gives special meaning to Luke's report that after his preaching to the rabbis in the temple, Jesus returned to Nazareth with his parents and advanced in wisdom and stature in divine and human favor (2:52).

Lecture 6:
Elijah, John the Baptist, and Zarathustra

Except for the depiction of Christ's resurrection, there is probably no scene in the New Testament so rich in mystery and numinosity as the Transfiguration, described by Matthew (17:1-8), and in the following words by Luke: "Jesus took with him Peter and James and John and went up on the mountain to pray. And while he was praying, the appearance of his face changed, and his clothes became dazzling white. Suddenly they saw two men, Moses and Elijah, talking to him" (9:28).

According to Steiner, Moses and Elijah are both richly textured figures in the evolution of the Hebrews and of humanity. Moses, who possessed the etheric body of Zarathustra, led the Hebrew people to a profound relationship to the external world, particularly to an articulated morality. Elijah, one of the great souls of ancient Israel, subsequently reincarnates in three awe-inspiring individuals: John the Baptist, Raphael, and Novalis. It is certainly edifying to consider that the figure who was seen by Peter, James, and John with Moses and the transfigured Christ was the same individuality as Jesus' cousin, John the Baptist. This same figure then brought to the dawn of the modern West the image of the Virgin Mary at the very center of Renaissance art. Then, in the midst of another period of intense spiritual creativity, this same great soul returned at the end of the eighteenth century as Novalis, the German Romantic mystic, scientist, poet, and devotee of Sophia, particularly in the form of the medieval Madonna.

Steiner's account of the work of the Nirmanakaya (manifest) Buddha in relation to John the Baptist is rather mysterious, but his conclusion at the end of this account is compelling: "Through these beings who appeared on the physical plane at the beginning of the Christian era, we begin to understand the unity of all religions and spiritual revelations to humankind." This proclamation follows from his statement that by listening to Buddha's actual teaching it is possible to hear that same teaching in the words of John the Baptist, namely, that it is not by conventional and comfortable practices of religion but rather by good deeds on one's own initiative that one will attain the fruits of repentance. That "the living bud of the sermon at Benares bloomed when John preached at the Jordan" is a vivid example of the larger truth, that in religion, as in all human affairs, truths evolve. "Because religions continue to evolve, we must look at each religion at the right point in human evolution and learn to understand its living aspects."

At the conclusion of this lecture, Rudolf Steiner indicates the singularity of the Zarathustra-Jesus from age twelve to thirty, and in the process gives a unique explanation for a text which has been used for many diverse purposes, some of them the source of mischief and suffering. Matthew, Mark, and Luke contain almost identical passages: "Then his mother and brethren came to him, but they could not reach him because of the crowd. And he was told, 'Your mother and your brothers are standing outside, wanting to see you.' But he said to them, 'My mother and my brothers are those who hear the word of God and do it'" (Luke 8:10, Matt. 12:46; Mark 3:31).

According to Steiner, Zarathustra-Jesus, in making this statement, was speaking from the esoteric fact of his having left the Matthew-Solomonic Jesus and united with the Luke-Nathanic Jesus, thereby leaving all links with his blood family. Steiner's reference to the Zarathustra-Jesus as having "to feel firsthand the impact of having no blood relationships" seems at odds with his earlier statement that his own blood mother, the mother of the deceased Matthew-Solomonic Jesus, still lived and later married the Joseph of the Luke-Nathanic Jesus. The mother of the Zarathustra-Jesus thereby became the step-mother of a son whose body was new to her but whose soul (Zarathustra) had inhabited her own blood son for the first twelve years of his life. Steiner does not indicate whether the stepmother of the Luke-Nathanic Jesus understood her son's, or stepson's, exquisitely crafted components, but in other lectures he does indicate that this mother became the object of Christian devotion.

In later lectures on the Gospels and on the Christ, Steiner indicates that the Zarathustra ego ("I") left Jesus of Nazareth just before the baptism and the descent into Jesus of Nazareth of the Christ. The etheric and astral bodies of Jesus of Nazareth at the descent of the Christ were those of Zarathustra combined with the physical body of the Nathan Jesus. If the ego of Zarathustra remained, and was joined by the ego of Christ, Steiner would be affirming the orthodox Christian (particularly Roman Catholic and Eastern Orthodox) teaching that Jesus Christ had two natures, two highest principles (whether referred to as soul, spirit, or "I"). It is clear that Steiner was not a Docetist: he did not consider Christ to have only a divine nature and, in effect, an illusory body. According to

Steiner, Christ entered a physical, etheric, and astral body. All of these suffered crucifixion and all but the physical body were resurrected. Steiner says that the physical body entered the etheric immediately after the crucifixion. The exact relationship of the ego of Zarathustra and the ego of Christ seems not entirely clear in these lectures, which are, after all, the first in which Steiner speaks of his astonishing realization of two Jesus families.

Steiner also indicates that the virginity of the mother of the Luke-Nathanic Jesus is true, but is not to be understood according to contemporary thinking and terminology. It is important to begin reflection on this mystery by acknowledging that the mother of the Luke Jesus received portions of the etheric body of Eve. This transmission is parallel to the transmission to the Luke-Nathanic Jesus of the part of the etheric body that incarnated as Adam. In Lecture Four, Steiner stated, "The Adam soul that existed before the Fall appears again in the [Nathanic] boy Jesus." (In referring to Christ as the Second Adam, it would seem that Paul understood a special relationship of Jesus to Adam, though Steiner does not indicate whether on the basis of his esoteric research Paul recognized in Jesus the etheric body of Adam. It seems obvious enough that Paul had an experience of the etheric and astral body — for example as a result of his experience of the resurrected Christ on the road to Damascus — but this does not establish whether Paul actually had access to the concepts "etheric" and "astral.")

Similarly, the mother of the Luke child received portions of the etheric body of Eve, also prior to Eve's experience in the event referred to in Genesis as the Fall. (According to Steiner, the Fall was indeed a separation from the garden of divine consciousness, but was equally an embrace of the knowledge of the tree of good and evil — a necessary and positive step in the evolution of humanity toward eventual attainment of love and freedom.)

The soul of the mother of the Luke-Jesus was virginal with respect both to her freedom from the effects of the Fall and also to the manner by which she conceived. In his important essay, "The Mystery of Mary in Body, Soul, and Spirit,"[2] Emil Bock, following Steiner, explains that Mary conceived in a way that resembled the process of conception in a primordial, Edenic time. Bock notes that "virginal" does not necessarily mean without participation of a father but rather that the conception that took place within Mary was virginal. By this account, the presumed impregnation by Joseph would have been without the engagement of her body with the emotional or physical consciousness that came about as a result of the Fall.

The mother of the Matthew-Solomon Jesus, by contrast, gave birth to her Jesus in the usual manner. Steiner also states that at the baptism of Jesus, the soul of the virginal Luke mother entered the soul of the Matthew mother (who was the mother of the children referred to as Jesus's brothers and sisters in Mark 6:3), thereby providing a basis for the Christian belief that the mother of Jesus was indeed virginal at the birth and in later life. The joining of the soul of the Luke mother to the Matthew mother furthermore united in one being the exquisite range of functions and ideals attributed to Mary in medieval and Renaissance Christianity. The topic of the mother of Jesus in Steiner's thought and in the New Testament, esoterically considered, warrants reverent in-depth research.

Lecture 7:
Christ, The Great Mystery of Earth Evolution

In the seventh lecture, Steiner continues his account of great figures who contributed to the formation of Jesus and to the evolution of humanity, particularly Zarathustra and Moses. This lecture also contains Steiner's description of the development of the Luke Jesus child according to the seven-year cycle of growth now familiar to readers of Steiner's books on the Waldorf approach to education, on human development and on the evolution of consciousness. Steiner uses the seven-year cycle of growth in many contexts. Here is a sketch of the components; proper use will depend on the context.

Age in years	Development of body/soul	Characteristic capacity
1-7	Physical body	Willing, especially for the good
8-14	Etheric body	Feeling, especially for the beautiful
15-21	Astral body	Thinking, especially the truth
22-28	Sentient soul	Inspired thinking
29-35	Intellectual soul	Analytic thinking
36-42	Consciousness soul	Potential for warm and will-filled thinking

Before the Christ descended to the earth to begin life as a human being joined to the exquisitely prepared body and soul of Jesus of Nazareth, he showed himself to Moses in the light of the burning bush, in the announcement of his name, "I AM," and in the lightning flame on Mount Sinai. The Light of Christ was also seen by his great collaborator, Zarathustra, who referred to Christ as Ahura Mazda. According to Steiner, Zarathustra in effect said, "Look up to Ahura Mazda, to see how he reveals himself in the physical garments of light and warmth, which conceal the divine Word of creation that is approaching the earth."

Then Steiner turns to the Baptism of Jesus, which he considers to be the beginning of the most decisive event in all human history. He refers to this event in his most lofty and definitive mantric verse, the Foundation Stone Meditation:

> At the turning point of time
> The Spirit-light of the world
> Entered the stream of existence.
> Darkness of night had ceased its reign;
> Day-radiant light shone forth in human souls:
> Light that gives warmth to simple shepherds' hearts;
> Light that enlightens the wise heads of kings.

"The Spirit-light of the world" is the divine being called Vishva Karman by the ancient Indian *rishis* and Ahura Mazda by Zarathustra. Steiner refers to this being as the Sun Being and as Christ, and, following the Gospel of John, as the Logos and the "I AM." Steiner then turns to "one of the greatest mysteries in earthly evolution," the relation of this Being — Vishva Karman, Ahura Mazda, Logos, Christ — to the bodhisattvas and to Buddha. Steiner depicts a lodge of twelve bodhisattvas, including the one who became Buddha in the sixth century B.C., as having responsibility for all of earth evolution: "As teachers, they inspire specific faculties that human beings must acquire." At the center of this lodge of twelve is a thirteenth — a being who "radiates the substance of wisdom itself." The following paragraph is at the center of Steiner's account of the evolution of consciousness, and the essence of his understanding of and relation to Christ:

> The baptism in the Jordan, therefore, represents the point in human evolution when spiritual substance itself, the heavenly thirteenth being, appeared on earth. All other beings, both bodhisattvas and buddhas, taught about this being, and mighty preparations were required so that he could descend into a human body. This is the mystery of the baptism in the Jordan. The Gospels describe Vishva Karman, or Ahura Mazda, now called the Christ, in the body of the Nathanic Jesus. This being was to spend three years on earth as a human among humans, inhabiting a time-tested earthly entity with the thirty years of experience we described earlier. The Nathanic Jesus was irradiated and pervaded by a being who had previously been clothed in the radiant, warming sun rays shining down from the cosmos, a being who had left Earth when the Sun separated from it.

Lecture 8:
Illness and Healing in Luke and in the Evolution of Consciousness

The eighth lecture represents a sharp departure from the previous seven lectures, all of which are concerned with the collaborative contributions of higher beings. This lecture focuses on the history of illness and healing, on a parable and on two miracle cures found in Luke. Because Steiner's account of the evolution of consciousness is so vast, covering eons and epochs, it can sometimes seem abstract and removed from the experience of a modern person. His account of the evolution of illness — or the changing kinds of illnesses from one epoch to the next — can bring the account into sharp and immediately relevant focus. This survey of illness is particularly appropriate in the Gospel written by a physician with a special interest in cures. It is also a valuable way to understand Steiner's repeated emphasis on the comprehensive changes that mark transitions from one epoch to the next.

When reading any of Steiner's lectures that refer to historical epochs, it is important to keep in mind the exact order and general characterization of each epoch under discussion. In this lecture, Steiner discusses six of the seven epochs dating from the eighth millennium B.C. far into the future. He discusses illness and healing in the following time frames from the set of seven following the sinking of Atlantis to the fifth post-Atlantean, or current epoch, with a brief mention of the sixth post-Atlantean epoch, which will be next:

Post-Atlantean Epoch	Dates	Development of soul, body
Ancient Indian	8th-6th millennium B.C.	Etheric body
Ancient Persian	6th-3rd millennium B.C.	Astral body
Egypto-Hebraic	3rd millennium-8th century B.C.	Sentient (participatory, inspired) soul

Post-Atlantean Epoch	Dates	Development of soul, body
Greco-Roman-Christian	8th century B.C.–15th century A.D.	Intellectual soul
European-American	15th century–36th century A.D.	Consciousness (potentially warm) soul

This sequence proceeds in two directions: each age brings a loss of spiritual consciousness and spiritual knowledge and a corresponding increase in intelligence, physicality, and the possibility of freedom and love.

An understanding of the evolution of consciousness along these lines provides the context for Steiner's claim that Buddha and Christ had to incarnate exactly when they did. If Buddha were to come to earth in the present age, he would not be able to teach the eightfold path. If Christ had not incarnated in the present age, he would not have been able to work the miraculous cures that he did. Steiner forthrightly states that all modern teachings, such as those of Kant (against whom Steiner struggled in his epistemological works), are "elementary and fragmentary in comparison to the comprehensive principles of the eightfold path." The teachings of Buddha came as a deed; it will only be in the next epoch that human beings will be able to experience that deed in their own souls.

Lecture 9:
Christ and Maitreya Buddha

Steiner characterizes the current epoch in the evolution of consciousness as a time when development of a way of thinking characterized by love and will is necessary in all aspects of human inquiry, including inquiry concerning the Bible. Throughout his books and lectures, Steiner insists repeatedly that the time of belief should be past, and that it is time for spiritual knowledge, especially with respect to the revelations hidden in the Bible. Steiner states that if modern humanity does not develop the ability to read the truths hidden in the Bible, the Bible itself will be ignored and will become ever more inaccessible. What is needed, then, is an approach to the scriptures at the levels of imagination, inspiration, and intuition, as described in the first lecture. Even these three levels of spiritual knowledge will not necessarily or readily extend Steiner's clairvoyant research. They can, however, enable individuals and groups to begin to develop the spiritual knowledge needed for the present time, and begin to access the spiritual events and teachings revealed in the Bible and in esoteric research such as is found in Steiner's volumes.

By explicating the parable of the unjust steward,[3] Steiner introduces the idea that it is impossible to serve two masters, particularly when one is God and the other Mammon (the god of riches). He then shifts the meaning to refer to a master of the past and a master for the future: "When it persists into later times, everything that was right in times past eventually becomes an obstacle to later evolution."

Of far greater importance than this not particularly illuminating exegesis of the parable of the unjust steward is Steiner's use of the past and present with respect to Buddha and Christ. In this lecture Steiner first states a position which he will repeat in other lectures from 1909-13:

> The Buddha gave humankind knowledge of love and compassion, and when we have completely transformed our astral bodies through the eightfold path, we will know everything we need to know about the law of this path.

There is a difference, however, between wisdom, knowledge, or thoughts and an active, living force. There is a difference between knowing what an I should be like and imbuing ourselves with a living force that can then flow from the I into the entire world, as the force emanating from the Christ influenced the astral, etheric, and physical bodies of those around him. Humankind learned the content of the doctrine of compassion and love through the contribution of the great Buddha. In contrast, the Christ's contribution is not a doctrine but a living force. He sacrificed himself and descended to earth to pervade not only the astral body but also the I, teaching it to exude the substance of love. The Christ brought to earth love's substantial, living content, not merely its wise content. This is the essence of his mission.

Lecture 10:
The Mystery of Golgotha as a New Form of Initiation

As Steiner stated in the ninth lecture that it will not be until far in the future that human beings will be able to develop the soul capacity necessary for a full realization of the eightfold path of Buddha, in the tenth lecture he indicates that humanity has not been able to find in the biblical and Christian message the double truth of karma and rebirth. The Bible, and particularly a teaching such as the Beatitudes, is an important means of preparation for that eventual realization. Another preparation for future development of spiritual capacities is the initiation of the young man of Nain: unlike the cure of Jairus's daughter and the hemorrhaging woman (discussed in the previous lecture), Steiner reports that the young man of Nain was initiated by Christ, as was Lazarus,[4] and reincarnated as a teacher of Christianity.

Steiner then presents examples of three forms of the initiation process, or the evolution of initiation in three stages: Jonah's experience "in the whale" represents the first kind of initiation, one in which the initiates bore upon themselves "the sign of Jonah," and were able to testify concerning the spiritual world; that of King Solomon, to whom the spiritual world revealed itself, represents a second form of initiation; and a third form, exemplified by the experience of the transfiguration of Christ as witnessed by Peter, James, and John. The transfiguration event, as described by Matthew and Mark as well as by Luke, indicates that the disciples were spiritually unprepared to experience Christ in his full radiance. At the end of the three years that Christ Jesus spent on earth, he performed a series of deeds that Steiner refers to as the Mystery of Golgotha, a mystery solemn and sublime, which prospectively entails a new form of initiation for all of humanity. The Mystery of Golgotha, then, is nothing less than "an initiation transferred to the stage of world history."

It is the particular contribution of the Gospel of Luke to depict "the outpouring of love that forgives even the most terrible offense in the physical world." The Gospel of Luke, particularly by its depiction of the crucifixion, teaches the union in Christ, and in the ideal of life in Christ, of faith, love, and hope. Steiner concludes this lofty and ennobling set of ten lectures with the plea that his listeners — and now by implication his readers — attend to the Gospel of Luke, and particularly to its ability to endow "human souls with the warm love that allows peace to dwell on earth." Steiner refers to this love as "the most exquisite reflection of divine mysteries."

Notes

1. A.L. Herman, *An Introduction to Indian Thought* (Englewood Cliffs, N.J.: Prentice Hall, 1976), p. 179.

2. *The Golden Blade* (1986), pp. 17–35.

3. Steiner's impatient insistence that the Greek *eis ten genean* be translated "in their own way" has not been followed by any of the standard translations into English.

4. See Rudolf Steiner, *The Gospel of St. John* (New York: Anthroposophic Press, 1962), lecture 4.

GUIDE TO FURTHER READING

Lecture Cycles by Rudolf Steiner

The Apocalypse of St. John: Lectures on the Book of Revelation. Nuremberg, June 17-30, 1908. Translated by M. Cotterell and J. Collis. London: Rudolf Steiner Press, 1977.

Background to the Gospel of St. Mark. October 17, 1910–June 10, 1911. Translated by E.H. Goddard and D.S. Osmond. London: Rudolf Steiner Press, 1968.

The Fifth Gospel. Oslo, October 1-6 and Cologne, December 17-18, 1913. Translated by C. Davy and D.S. Osmond. London: Rudolf Steiner Press, 1968.

The Gospel of St. John. May 18-31, 1908. Translated by Maud Monges. New York: Anthroposophic Press, 1962.

The Gospel of St. John and Its Relation to the Other Gospels. June 24–July 7, 1909. Translated by Samuel and Loni Lockwood, revised by Maria St. Goar. Edited by Stewart C. Easton. New York: Anthroposophic Press, 1982.

The Gospel of St. Mark. Basel, September 15-24, 1912. Translated by Erna McArthur. New York: Anthroposophic Press, 1950.

The Gospel of St. Matthew. Berne, September 1-12, 1910. Translated by Dorothy Osmond and Mildred Kirkcaldy. London: Rudolf Steiner Press, 1965.

Books Informed by Rudolf Steiner's Research

Bock, Emil. *The Apocalypse of St. John.* Translated by Alfred Heidenreich. Edinburgh: Floris Books, 1957.

———. *The Childhood of Jesus: The Unknown Years.* Translated by Maria St. Goar. Edinburgh: Floris Books, 1980.

———. *Genesis: Creation and the Patriarchs.* Translated by Maria St. Goar. Edinburgh: Floris Books, 1983.

———. *Moses: From the Mysteries of Egypt to the Judges of Israel.* Translated by Maria St. Goar. Edinburgh: Floris Books, 1986.

———. *The Three Years: The Life of Christ between Baptism and Ascension.* Edinburgh: Floris Books, 1955.

Frieling, Rudolf. *New Testament Studies*. Edited by Tony Jacobs-Brown. Edinburgh: Floris Books, 1994.

Smith, Edward Reaugh. *The Burning Bush: Rudolf Steiner, Anthroposophy, and the Holy Scriptures: An Anthroposophical Commentary on the Bible: Terms and Phrases*. Volume 1. Hudson, N.Y.: Anthroposophic Press, 1997.

——— . *The Incredible Births of Jesus*. Hudson, N.Y.: Anthroposophic Press, 1998.

Books by Contemporary New Testament Scholars

Borg, Marcus. *Jesus: A New Vision*. San Francisco: HarperSanFrancisco, 1987.

——— . *Meeting Jesus for the First Time*. San Francisco: HarperSanFrancisco, 1994.

Brown, Raymond E. *The Birth of the Messiah: A Commentary on the Infancy Narratives in Matthew and Luke*. New York: Doubleday Image, 1977.

Crossan, John Dominic. *The Historical Jesus: The Life of a Mediterranean Jewish Peasant*. San Francisco: HarperSanFrancisco, 1991.

——— . *Jesus: A Revolutionary Biography*. San Francisco: HarperSanFrancisco, 1994.

Funk, Robert, and Roy Hoover, eds. *The Five Gospels*. New York: Macmillan, 1993.

About this Edition

In these lectures on the Luke Gospel, which deal primarily with events leading up to the great Christ event, Rudolf Steiner speaks to members in detail about the two Jesus children for the first time. Hella Wiesberger listed additional lectures with important comments on the two Jesus children in *Nachrichten der Rudolf Steiner-Nachlaßverwaltung* ("News from the Rudolf Steiner Archives"), now *Beiträge zur Rudolf Steiner Gesamtausgabe* ("Articles about Rudolf Steiner's Complete Works"), no. 8, Christmas 1962, p. 36. Rudolf Steiner's first published discussion of this subject appeared in 1911 in *The Spiritual Guidance of the Individual and Humanity*, Hudson, N.Y.: Anthroposophic Press, 1992 (GA 15, *Die Geistige Führung des Menschen und der Menschheit*). See also Adolf Arenson's summary of Rudolf Steiner's research on the two Jesus children in *Die Kindheitsgeschichte Jesu. Die beiden Jesusknaben* ("The Biography of the Boy Jesus: The Two Jesus Children"), Stuttgart, 1921; Emil Bock's account in *Kindheit und Jugend Jesu* ("The Childhood and Adolescence of Jesus"), Stuttgart 1939 (fifth ed. 1980); and Hella Krause-Zimmer's *Die Zwei Jesusknaben in der bildenden Kunst* ("The Two Jesus Children in the Fine Arts"), second ed., Stuttgart 1977.

For more information on Zarathustra-Nazarathos, see Rudolf Steiner's lectures in Berlin on November 9, 1909 (in *Deeper Secrets of Human History in the Light of the Gospel of St. Matthew*, London: Anthroposophical Publishing Co., 1957) and in Munich on December 7, 1909. For more about the life and teachings of the Buddha, see Rudolf Steiner's lectures in Berlin on October 11 and 18, 1909, given shortly after this cycle in Basel. All of these lectures are included in GA 117, *Die*

Tieferen Geheimnisse des Menschheitswerden im Lichte der Evangelien ("The Deeper Mysteries of Humankind's Evolution as Illumined by the Gospels"). Dornach, Switzerland: Verlag der Rudolf Steiners Nachlassverwaltung, 1966.

The translation of this volume of lectures on the Luke Gospel is based on the sixth German edition, which incorporates a few changes derived from originals not available when the fifth edition was published. All German editions were based on Walter Vegelahn's transcription of his original shorthand notes, which have not been preserved.

In most cases, Gospel passages quoted by Rudolf Steiner were taken from Luther's translation of the Bible into German. The English translation follows the Revised Standard Version unless otherwise noted.

Marie Steiner's preface to earlier German editions of these lectures is now included in volume 1 of her collected works, *Die Anthroposophie Rudolf Steiners. Gesammelte Vorworte zu Erstveröffentlichungen von Werken Rudolf Steiners* ("Rudolf Steiner's Anthroposophy: Collected Prefaces to First Editions of Rudolf Steiner's Works"), Dornach 1967.